BOYMANS-VAN BEUNINGEN MUSEUM

The Boymans-van Beuningen
Museum from the garden

Erratum

Tot onze spijt is op pagina 123 het schilderij '1897' van Georg Baselitz ondersteboven gereproduceerd.

We regret that due to a reproduction error on p. 123, Georg Baselitz' painting '1897' is reproduced upside-down.

Wir bedauern, dass durch ein technisches Versehen das Gemälde '1897' von Georg Baselitz auf Seite 123 verkehrt herum abgebildet wurde.

A notre grand regret, le tableau '1897' de Georg Baselitz a été represented à l'envers à la page 123.

Hanneke de Man

Boymans-van Beuningen Museum

SCALA BOOKS

© Scala Publications Limited/Boymans-van Beuningen Museum Rotterdam
© Text Hanneke de Man

© Photos Boymans-van Beuningen Museum Rotterdam

First published in 1993 by
Scala Publications Ltd
26 Litchfield Street
London WC2H 9NJ

Distributed in the USA and Canada by
Rizzoli International Publications, Inc.
300 Park Avenue South
New York
NY 10010

ISBN 1 870248 95 3 (hardback)

Designed by Alan Bartram
Translated from Dutch by Ruth Koenig
Edited by Jane Havell
Photographs by Tom Haartsen, Jannes Linders, Dick Wolters
Produced by Scala Publications Ltd
Typeset by August Filmsetting, St Helens, England
Printed and bound by Snoeck Ducaju & Zoon N.V., Ghent, Belgium

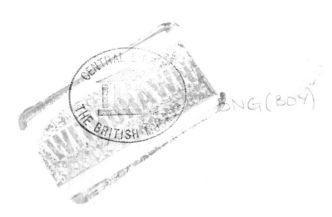

Contents

Foreword

The tall tower of the Boymans-van Beuningen Museum has lost little of its attraction, despite having had to compete with Rotterdam's spectacular high-rise buildings for the past few decades. When the building was opened in 1935, however, this landmark bore the brunt of criticism levelled at the museum for 'its unseemly elevation above the sober reality of everyday life'. The museum's history is nonetheless indissolubly linked with Rotterdam's function as a port. Without the city's economic activity, the development of the Boymans-van Beuningen Museum would have taken quite a different course.

The museum is characterized by its great variety. Besides Pieter Bruegel's *Tower of Babel* and Rembrandt's *Titus*, visitors may see Kandinsky's *Lyrisches* and Dali's *Impressions d'Afrique*. A small Italian Renaissance bronze lives under the same roof as the colossal *Waxing Arcs* by Richard Serra. A medieval cooking-pot and a Tupperware plastic jar rub shoulders with an ornate Nautilus cup and a skilfully cut glass. Then there are the rich contents of the print room, with its thousands of drawings and prints dating from the Middle Ages to the present, an inexhaustible source for changing exhibitions.

This book is a most welcome means of introducing the public to our museum, its history and varied collections. My thanks to the author Hanneke de Man and to Charlotte Groenewold, Andrea Svedlin and Charlotte Wiethoff for their assistance. Last but not least, I wish to express my gratitude to Scala Books for this opportunity to put our museum in the ranks of the many important museums from all over Europe featured in this series.

WIM CROUWEL
Director, Boymans-van Beuningen Museum

Introduction

Unlike Amsterdam, where in 1808 King Louis Napoleon launched the initiative for a Royal Museum – the precursor of the Rijksmuseum – and unlike The Hague, where King William I's Royal Picture Gallery was opened to the public in 1820, Rotterdam lacked an important public art collection at the beginning of the nineteenth century.

The occasional group portrait in the possession of the municipal council and a sixteenth-century copy of Holbein's portrait of Rotterdam's most illustrious son, Desiderius Erasmus, hardly merited the erection of a museum of art. The first opportunity presented itself when the Utrecht lawyer F. J. O. Boijmans (1767-1847) left his collection of paintings, prints, drawings and porcelain to the City of Rotterdam on condition that these treasures be suitably housed.

On 3 July 1849, unattended by any festivities, the Boymans Museum opened in the Schielandshuis, a baroque-classicist building by Pieter Post and Jacob Lois, dating from 1662-65, purchased by Rotterdam Council expressly for the purpose (today it houses the Historical Museum). The works of art were displayed on the top floor, the ground floor being occupied by an art school. The museum got off to a sluggish start. In 1852 A. J. Lamme (1812-1900) was appointed as the first, unsalaried, director; of nearly 1200 paintings in the original collection, he deemed only 406 to be of sufficiently high quality to be worth retaining, and a large number of works were sold to pay for new ones. However, instead of increasing, the collection was sadly, and dramatically, diminished: a fire in the night of 15 February 1864 destroyed two-thirds of the paintings, half the drawings and virtually all the prints and porcelain.

There was, in any case, little scope for growth. In keeping with national policy, which did not regard art as a government issue, Rotterdam's priorities were elsewhere. The council twice turned down offers which would immediately have established the museum's international status, claiming to 'lack the freedom to spend money destined merely for pleasure'. In 1845, during negotiations with F. J. O. Boijmans, the council had declined the far superior collection of J. G. Baron Verstolk van Soelen, for many years the Dutch envoy in St Petersburg and until 1841 the Minister of Foreign Affairs. In 1869 it passed up another unique opportunity when the heirs of Dirk Vis Blokhuyzen, a former member of the museum board, offered his collection for next to nothing. Despite the efforts of Rotterdam citizens to retain this splendid collection – which included masterpieces by Rembrandt, Ter Borch, Frans Hals and Vermeer – the council was adamant. Shortly afterwards it was auctioned in Paris. Even then, Rotterdam made no bids for the important pieces, so that Vermeer's celebrated *Lacemaker* went to the Louvre in Paris for 3,635 guilders.

Successes, however, compensated for such setbacks. With the insurance compensation for the fire a number of pieces were bought, which have become the highlights of today's collection, among them Rembrandt's *Concord of the State*, *Portrait of a Standing Man* by Frans Hals and Jan van Scorel's *Portrait of a Young Scholar*. In addition, a bequest enabled the purchase of Pieter Jansz Saenredam's *St Mary's Square and St Mary's Church* for the sum, incredible by today's standards, of only 1,150 guilders.

Although the council was reluctant to provide financial support, it did supply a basis for the museum's growth in other ways. Rotterdam's development as a port, strongly boosted by the construction of the Nieuwe Waterweg in 1869, produced new patrons whose wealth derived from trade and shipping.

Dr F. Schmidt-Degener (1882-1941), who became the director of the museum in 1908, and Dr D. Hannema (1896-1984), who succeeded him in 1921, forged firm links with wealthy Rotterdam citizens. Dirk Hannema, in particular, motivated several collectors to 'promote the museum for the lasting benefit of the community'. Between 1910 and World War I the museum developed at a tremendous pace, expanding its holdings of both old and modern masters, prints, drawings and applied art. In 1910 Dr E. van Rijckevorsel (1845-1928) made a gift of his collection of antique glass and porcelain, the beginning of a series of donations and bequests which made the applied art department one of the finest in the country. Of the many private benefactors, J. P. van der Schilden (1851-1925) deserves special mention. A Rotterdam furniture manufacturer, he had amassed a renowned collection of pottery and old and modern silver by the end of the nineteenth century. He was variously involved in museum affairs, and was a member of the Board of Trustees. When he died in 1925 he bequeathed to Boymans not only his collection of decorative art and paintings of the Hague School but also his fortune, from which the museum bought Hieronymus Bosch's famous *Prodigal Son* in 1931.

There was ample compensation, too, for the losses in the drawing and print departments, which became even better off than before. In 1923 the museum acquired the prints and drawings collected by A. J. Domela Nieuwenhuis (1850-1935), brother of the well-known Frisian anarchist Ferdinand Domela Nieuwenhuis. In 1935 the museum received on loan the superb collection of drawings belonging to the banker Franz Koenigs (1881-1941), along with paintings by Hieronymus Bosch and Peter Paul Rubens.

Interior of the Schielandshuis

It was, however, in the field of old master paintings that the museum attained particular distinction during this period. Largely responsible for this development were D. G. van Beuningen (1877-1955) and Willem van der Vorm (1873-1957), two shipping magnates who enjoyed a monopoly on Holland's coal trade with Germany and England. Thanks to director Hannema's powers of persuasion and the generosity of the two tycoons, the museum was able to make numerous purchases.

D. G. van Beuningen's first donation in 1916 was followed by many more, culminating in 1933 with the gift of six oil sketches from Rubens' *Achilles* series. Van der Vorm, too, funded several acquisitions. In 1927 he provided a

considerable sum for the purchase of Emanuel de Witte's large *Church Interior*, and in 1936 he presented Saenredam's *St Laurence's Church in Alkmaar*. Dirk Hannema advised Willem van der Vorm about building up his own collection, and the latter reciprocated by organizing the funding of acquisitions for the museum, which were often a problem to finance. For instance, van der Vorm was a founder-member of the Museum Boymans Foundation in 1939, an occasion he marked by presenting Gerrit Dou's *Quack*. The Foundation took prompt action to procure the portrait of Rembrandt's son Titus, which was eventually bought with the support of '120 Friends of the Museum'.

Thanks to these developments, Boymans grew into a

Drawing of the Schielandshuis two
days after the fire of 1864

museum which aspired to vie with the Mauritshuis and the
Rijksmuseum. To satisfy such ambitions more spacious
accommodation, better suited to the museum's specific
requirements, was needed. In 1928 Hannema succeeded in
persuading the council to finance a new building from the
Burger legacy, bequeathed to the city of Rotterdam by
Gerardus Willem Burger in 1916. The chosen location was
called Hoboken's Ground, a site near the centre of town
which the city already owned.

A design was commissioned from the municipal architect,
A. van der Steur (1893-1953). He and Hannema inspected a
number of European museums and in close collaboration
drew up a plan in which the galleries were arranged around

two courtyards. The ground floor was reserved for applied
art, the first floor for paintings. On entering the building,
visitors immediately had a monumental view of paintings on
the upper floor through an opening, an architectural device
which subtly accentuated the focus of the collection.

The variously sized galleries reflected the structure of the
collection. Three sets of small rooms, alternating with larger
galleries, emphasised the 'domestic' nature of many of the
paintings. A slightly domed gallery was destined for the
sculptures. A long room next to the entrance was to
accommodate changing exhibitions. These variations in shape
and size, the architectural openings and the occasional
glimpses of the surrounding park were deliberately

9

The Boymans-van Beuningen
Museum from the front

introduced to 'prevent visitors from tiring too easily'.
Lighting was an important factor, and detailed experiments
were carried out with an ingenious skylight construction.

Although one of the prime considerations was to create as
neutral an environment as possible for the works of art, one is
struck by the subtle detailing of the interior, which features
various kinds of marble and oak panelling. The façade is
brick combined with stone, topped by a copper roof. A tower
surmounted by a tall lantern not only accentuates the
entrance but gives the museum the status of a landmark.

The festive inauguration of the building on 6 July 1935 was
enhanced by an exhibition titled 'Vermeer, origin and
influence', followed a year later by 'Hieronymus Bosch and
the North-Netherlandish Primitives', two internationally
prestigious shows. All this activity was brought to an abrupt
halt by the outbreak of World War II. That the museum
survived the bombardment of May 1940 was a miracle,

though it did suffer a certain amount of damage two years
later. The works of art, stored in air-raid shelters in various
parts of the country, came through the war unscathed.

In 1945 Hannema had to resign because of his political
attitude during the war. He was succeeded in 1950 by
J. C. Ebbinge Wubben (b.1915), who had joined the staff as
curator of the print room in 1941. Under his directorship the
museum acquired a number of important private collections.
In 1951 Dr J. C. J. Bierens de Haan (1867-1951) bequeathed his
large collection of prints. The acquisition of D. G. van
Beuningen's collection in 1958 crowned the relationship
between the collector and the museum; to underline this
auspicious event, the museum's name was changed to the
Boymans-van Beuningen Museum. The arrival of the van
Beuningen collection meant that more space was needed,
while a growing number of exhibitions and an increased
interest in modern art made expansion even more pressing.

Entrance to the 1935 building

Galleries

The museum's interest in modern art was not new. Ever since the end of the nineteenth century works by contemporary artists had been making their way into the collection. The then director, P. Haverkorn van Rijsewijk (1839-1919), championed the artists of the Hague School, in those days still the subject of controversy. It was under his directorship, in 1903, that 26 Rotterdam art-lovers donated van Gogh's *Lane of Poplars near Nuenen*, the artist's first painting to grace a Dutch public collection. Although there was no deliberate acquisition policy for modern art, important contemporary works continued to swell the collection in the years that followed. In 1929, for instance, a few unnamed friends of Mondrian presented his *Composition in Yellow and Blue*, painted that same year. An extremely valuable loan from one of the most progressive collectors of the period, Marie Tak van Poortvliet, was converted into a bequest in 1936, ensuring the museum's permanent ownership of Kandinsky's *Lyrisches*, Franz Marc's *Lamb* and Feininger's *Ober Weimar*. Dirk Hannema had a deep personal commitment to modern art, not only presenting a number of pieces himself, but also making use of his contacts with wealthy Rotterdam citizens with a view to buying works.

Even so, not until the 1950s was modern art purchased on a larger scale. 1950 was a historic year: Ebbinge Wubben bought his first important modern work, Kokoschka's *Mandril* of 1926. He had to convince the Board of Trustees first, though: D. G. van Beuningen consented only on condition that he would never have to set eyes on the picture.

The desire to give modern art a proper place in the museum led to the birth of an independent modern art department in 1963. Mrs R. Hammacher-van den Brande was its first curator. From the outset the impossibility of filling gaps in the modern collection was quite clear. Nevertheless, two exceptions were made. When New York's Guggenheim Museum auctioned some of its Kandinskys in 1964, Boymans bought a group of eleven works. The second exception was surrealist art, a movement that was poorly represented in the Netherlands and to which the museum drew attention in a series of exhibitions.

Plans to expand the museum dated from the war period, and were resumed in peacetime. In 1964 the council approved the choice of architect A. Bodon (1906-1993) to design the extension, but it was 1972 before the new wing was finished. Eight years of designing and preparations had one advantage, however: the definitive plan took account of the growing importance of the modern art department and of the special requirements of its exhibitions.

It was decided to have a few large, flexible rooms which could be divided up in a variety of ways by movable partitions. The first floor is top-lit. The large wall areas are broken by a few windows, the largest of which commands a splendid view of the gardens. The ground-floor galleries are lit from the sides; enclosed in the centre is a print room, illuminated only by artificial light. The courtyard orientation of the 1935 building gave the street façade an almost unapproachably introverted air. In the new wing, by contrast, in accordance with current ideas about a museum's function, an attempt was made to involve passers-by in what was going on inside by means of a long glass façade; in 1991 this was replaced by a new main entrance, flanked by a shop and restaurant. In spite of obvious differences between the two architects' backgrounds and between former and current views as to the function of a museum, Bodon united the two tracts of the building well, partly by his use of brickwork.

In 1978 J. C. Ebbinge Wubben was succeeded by Dr W. A. L. Beeren (*b*.1928). Modern art came in for even more attention, and under Wim Beeren's directorship Boymans has established its reputation as a major museum of modern art. As well as introducing the very latest works, Beeren focused on five artists whom he regards as crucial to today's art: Joseph Beuys, Bruce Nauman, Claes Oldenburg, Andy Warhol and Walter De Maria. In order to cement the relationship between the museum and these artists, he invited them to make works especially for Boymans. In the case of Beuys the upshot, as well as the purchase of a major work, was a two-day discussion which took place in the museum in 1980. Walter De Maria made a floor-piece for the large central gallery of the new wing, and Claes Oldenburg's *Screw Arch* series seeks a link with Rotterdam.

Although the growth of the collection has been largely financed with municipal funds since the 1950s, and private patronage has gradually given way to industrial sponsorship, private collectors have continued to make significant contributions in recent decades.

When the new wing opened in 1972, the museum acquired on a long loan the Willem van der Vorm collection, administered by a foundation, which brought in top-ranking pieces by van Dyck, Ter Borch, Metsu and Jan Steen. In 1975 the art historian Vitale Bloch (1900-1975) bequeathed his small but exquisite collection of paintings and drawings.

More recently, the large van Beuningen-de Vriese collection of pre-industrial utensils, accepted in 1981, prompted the museum to set its sights on the new territory of design. Despite the acquisition of A. J. G. Verster's collection of pewter utensils in 1955, the accent in the department of applied art had remained on decorative objects whose place in the museum depended on their artistic merit. The

1
The new wing, 1972

2
The van Beuningen-de Vriese
Pavilion, 1991

2

museum has now enlarged this area to cover the much wider field of design and industrial design, an aspect which has become more prominent under the aegis of Professor W. H. Crouwel (*b*.1928), who succeeded Wim Beeren as director in 1985.

The van Beuningen-de Vriese collection was initially transferred to the museum in instalments, starting in 1983, which took the form of a loan to be converted into a gift as soon as fitting conditions for its permanent display were created. This became possible in 1991, when the van Beuningen-de Vriese Pavilion, designed by H.J. Henket (born 1940) in close consultation with Wim Crouwel, was built on to the garden side of the museum. The collection of utensils is on show in the basement, whose closed character is appropriate to the exhibits, most of which were dug up during excavations. The upper gallery forms a stark contrast: its high degree of transparency results from the combination of glass and a silver-coloured steel roof and skeleton construction. Changing exhibitions of applied art and design are held in this gallery, which overlooks the museum garden, laid out in the 1930s.

In spite of the new wing and the pavilion, such a vast collection and varied exhibition programme continues to demand more space.

In 1993 there seems to be little to remind us of the museum's nineteenth-century origins, but nevertheless that is when the foundations were laid for the collection as it appears today. It boasts no monumental works of art from royal or municipal collections. The Boymans-van Beuningen Museum owes its holdings to the enthusiasm of private collectors who entrusted their wide-ranging collections to the museum, where they have found a home in four departments: Old Masters, Modern Art, Applied Art and Design, Prints and Drawings. Compared with other leading Dutch museums, it is the very diversity of those collections that has helped to form the specific character of the museum.

The van Beuningen-de Vriese Pavilion

Department of Old Masters

Frans Jacob Otto Boijmans (1767-1847)

Although Rotterdam may seem the obvious home for the Boymans Museum, Frans Jacob Otto Boijmans, unlike the many collectors who were to follow his example, had scarcely any links with the city. A physician's son born in Maastricht, Boijmans spent most of his life in Utrecht, where he studied law and was later, from 1818 to 1839, to preside as a judge. In 1788 he married a noblewoman, Arnoudina Elisabeth van Westreenen, who died only two years later; they had one son, Jan André, born in 1789. As was fitting among members of his social class, Boijmans appreciated and collected fine art. He was a member of Kunstliefde, founded in 1807 in Utrecht as 'a modern artists' society for drawing clothed models'. In the winter months he also gave talks on art appreciation, based on works in his own collection. Only in rare cases is it possible to trace the provenance of his paintings, drawings, prints, and Chinese and Saxe porcelain. Some items were most likely purchased on his travels, which took him to Paris and Brussels at regular intervals, to Berlin in 1805 and a year later to Rome for a time.

Around 1809, in order to pay his son the maternal portion to which he was entitled on coming of age, Boijmans decided to sell his collection. An attempt to dispose of it *en bloc* to the Royal Museum, later the Rijksmuseum, was unsuccessful. In 1811 he therefore organized a large auction in Amsterdam, with a catalogue listing 431 paintings and some 4,000 drawings. The results, however, were so disappointing that in the end Boijmans decided to keep the collection. After his son's premature death, he expanded it. As well as seventeenth-century Dutch art, he favoured landscapes and seascapes by contemporary painters, with some of whom he was personally acquainted. According to the Utrecht architect, painter and artists' biographer Christiaan Kramm (1797–1875), Boijmans was a single-minded collector: 'He had an insatiable desire to possess everything, and since he lived very simply, keeping but a single maidservant, his household was so frugal that all his money could go into art.'

Even later on, Boijmans seems to have found it hard to interest anyone in his collection. His offer to present it to the city of Utrecht in 1829 was declined. In the end it was his friendship with the mayor of Rotterdam, M.C. Bichon van IJsselmonde, that enabled the collection to be kept together after his death, in accordance with his wishes. In 1841 he offered it to Rotterdam on condition that the city provided suitable accommodation. The council accepted his offer the following year and purchased the seventeenth-century Schielandshuis to house the collection, but many years passed before Boijmans' intentions were realized. On 11 June 1847, only eight days before his death, he at last signed the documents, having reluctantly waived his stipulation that the city of Rotterdam should earmark an annual sum of 25,000 guilders for the purchase of contemporary art.

On 3 July 1849 the Boymans Museum opened its doors without any accompanying festivities. Of almost 1,200 paintings, the art dealer Arnoldus Lamme and his son Arie Johannes, the museum's first director, put barely 400 on show In 1853, 1854 and 1855, parts of Boijmans' collection were sold so that new purchases could be made. A large number of works were destroyed in a fire at the Schielandshuis in 1864: 300 paintings, 13 portfolios of drawings, nearly all the prints and all the porcelain. This disaster put paid to any hopes of forming a complete picture of the collector characterized by former director Schmidt Degener as 'an eighteenth-century man through and through …, a strange connoisseur with a few good and all the bad sides of his self-willed expertise: stinging pedantry, complete faith in the infallibility of his own judgement and a violent animosity towards those who dared to doubt the value of his art treasures.' This opinion should be seen in the proper perspective. It is to this collector that Rotterdam owes not only a museum but also such uncontested masterpieces as Fabritius's *Portrait of a Man*, Ruisdael's *Cornfield*, Philip Koninck's *Panoramic Landscape* and Steen's *Feast of St Nicholas*.

Daniel George van Beuningen (1877-1955)

When the museum acquired the van Beuningen collection in 1958, it was discovered that the collector kept a notebook in which he carefully recorded each purchase and its price, also making a note whenever he sold a work to improve the quality of his collection. The book is not only a valuable document for the history of the collection but also tells us something of its owner's character.

D. G., as he was usually called, was born in Utrecht in 1877. His father was H. A. van Beuningen, director of the Steenkolen Handels Vereniging, a coal trading company. Poor eyesight put paid to the boy's ambition of becoming a naval officer, and so he entered his father's firm and in 1900 was charged with setting up a branch in Rotterdam. In the hands of this ambitious young man, the company became the major coal trader with the Ruhr region and grew into an international concern with agencies in numerous ports.

D. G. started to realize his ambitions as a collector at an early age. With his first earnings he bought blue delftware in 1899, but soon became enamoured of painting. In keeping with current taste, he started with works of the Hague and the Barbizon Schools, but soon became interested in art unbounded by national borders or periods. He was one of the first collectors of late fifteenth- and early sixteenth-century

Portrait of F.J.O. Boijmans, pastel, 1788

D.G. van Beuningen, photograph, c1950

North and South Netherlandish art, the so-called 'primitives'. He also acquired a large number of seventeenth-century Dutch paintings, as well as works by French and Italian painters. His first purchase in the latter field, made in 1928, was a tremendous feather in his cap: *Child in a Landscape*, to this day the only Titian in any Dutch collection. Van Beuningen was less in sympathy with modern art, his interest going only as far as the Impressionists. His most modern purchase was an early Picasso inspired by Lautrec, a little painting which he presented to the museum when the new building was opened in 1935. It was only one of a succession of gifts to the museum, the first of which had been made in 1916. Van Beuningen rarely turned down a request for financial help, and Hannema in turn often advised the collector.

Van Beuningen had good contacts with several leading dealers at home and abroad. He was thus able to acquire a number of important pieces during the recession of the 1930s, including works from the Auspitz collection in Vienna and, shortly before the outbreak of World War II, the English Cook collection. During the war van Beuningen's large collection was moved from his Rotterdam residence to his country estate of Noorderheide in the Veluwe region, where the works were buried in wooden, zinc-lined crates. In 1945 they were disinterred in good condition, and most of them found a home in Noorderheide House, which van Beuningen had built on the heath near Vierhouten.

D. G. devoted the last decade of his life to his two ruling passions: nature and art. His home was filled from top to bottom with his beloved art treasures. He would enthusiastically show his many guests, who included prominent art historians, round the house. In the hall, along with other works, hung Titian's masterpiece; in the dining room, surrounded by primitives, were Bruegel's *Tower of Babel* and *The Three Maries at the Sepulchre* by the van Eyck brothers. The Italian masters were in the drawing room. The staircase, which was hung with oil sketches by Rubens, led up to the Impressionists and eighteenth-century French painters whose works graced the bedrooms.

This forceful personality died in 1955, leaving his collection to his children, who offered it to the city of Rotterdam in 1958 on condition that the council pay the death duties. The museum thus came into the possession of 189 paintings, 30 wooden sculptures and bronzes, five items of silverware by van Vianen and others, and 17 drawings; it also acquired the second half of its name, Boymans-van Beuningen.

Along with earlier gifts, including six oil sketches from Rubens' *Achilles* series and the major part of the Koenigs collection, the museum's holdings enjoy an international reputation, for which van Beuningen is largely responsible.

1 and 1A
Bishopric of Liège (c1415)
Norfolk Triptych
Panel, 33.2 × 59 cm
Coll. D. G. van Beuningen 1958;
inv. 2466
The *Norfolk Triptych*, named after
the Dukes of Norfolk who owned it
until 1930, is one of the oldest panels
in the museum's collection. Gold

leaf was used on the inside, plain oils
on the outside. An example of costly
workmanship, the small triptych was
intended for private devotions. On
the middle panel is a representation
of the Coronation of the Virgin,
underneath which is the Man of
Sorrows: Christ surrounded by the
instruments of the Passion. On
either side are numerous saints,

many of whom were venerated in
the Liège and Maastricht area. This
is one reason for assuming that the
triptych was painted in the Meuse
valley, the native region of the van
Eyck brothers.

1

2
**Jan van Eyck and Hubert van
Eyck (Maaseyck c1390 – Bruges
1441; Maaseyck c1370 – Ghent 1426)**
*The Three Maries at the Open
Sepulchre*, after 1430
Panel, 71.5 × 89 cm
Coll. D. G. van Beuningen 1958;
inv. 2449
This purchase by D. G. van Beuningen from the Cook collection
shortly before the outbreak of World
War II was one of his most spectacular and costly acquisitions. Simil-
arities in style and technique permit
the panel to be attributed to the
makers of the great altarpiece in St
Bavo's Cathedral in Ghent, the brothers Hubert and Jan van Eyck. The
depicted episode shows the three
Maries at the resurrected Christ's
open grave on Easter Morning.
Around the sepulchre, which is
rendered in slightly distorted perspective, three soldiers lie in a deep
sleep. One of them is wearing a
gleaming cuirass in which the surroundings are reflected. Illuminated

by the rising sun, the city of Jerusa-
lem stands out against the horizon in
a fairly accurate topographical
rendering. The landscape, the figures and the plants in the foreground are executed in minute
detail in a technique of layer upon
layer of paint.

3
**Master of the Gathering of the
Manna (c1476)**
Offering of the Jews
Panel, 69.5 × 51.5 cm
Acquired with the aid of the Eras-
mus Foundation, Rotterdam and the
Rembrandt Foundation 1951;
inv. 2439

4
Northern Netherlands (c1500)
Lamentation
Polychrome oak, height 56.5 cm
Gift of D. G. van Beuningen 1922;
inv. 1056

1A

4

Geertgen tot Sint Jans
(Leyden c1460/65 – Haarlem
c1490/95)
The Glorification of the Virgin
Panel, 24.5 × 18 cm
Coll. D. G. van Beuningen 1958;
inv. 2450
Against the night sky we see the
vision described by St John in the
Book of Revelation: 'a woman clothed with the sun, and the moon
under her feet.' The Madonna and
Child are surrounded by three rings
of angels. The two figures are bathed
in a warm glow which gradually
fades into the darkness, just catching
the almost transparent, music-
making angels in the outer ring. On
this little panel Geertgen has
depicted virtually the entire instru-
mentarium of his period in painstaking detail. This was not, of
course, a standard ensemble:
Geertgen introduced all these
instruments to swell the paeans of
the angels, who are conducted by
the Infant Jesus with his tinkling
bells.

I

2

Jacopo del Sellaio
(Florence 1441/42 – Florence 1493)
Orpheus and Eurydice
Panel, 60 × 150 cm
Coll. D. G. van Beuningen 1958;
inv. 2563
The story of Orpheus and Eurydice
is enacted in front of a charming
landscape. The depicted episode

shows Eurydice fleeing from the
advances of Aristaios, god of the
shepherds; she treads on a snake and
is fatally bitten. The oblong panel
was formerly the front board of an
Italian cassone, a chest in which
clothes and bedding were kept.
These chests were often given in
pairs to wealthy couples on their
marriage.

3

Master of the Annunciation of Aix
(active c1445)
The Prophet Isaiah
Panel, 101.5 × 68 cm
Coll. D. G. van Beuningen 1958;
inv. 2463

2

3

4

4
Lorenzo Costa(?)
(Ferrara c.1460 – Mantua 1535)
Portrait of Pietro Cenni
Panel, 42 × 32 cm
Coll. D. G. van Beuningen 1958;
inv. 2562

1
Hieronymus Bosch
(Bois-le-Duc *c*1450 – Bois-le-Duc 1516)
The Vagabond
Panel, diameter 64.6 cm
Acquired with the aid of the J. P. van der Schilden Bequest, the Rembrandt Foundation and Friends of the Museum 1931; inv. 1079
Although Hieronymus Bosch never left Bois-le-Duc, his fame spread far beyond his native city. Philip II of Spain, for instance, was an avid collector of his work, and the Prado in Madrid houses many of his most imposing altarpieces. The Boymans-van Beuningen Museum is the only Dutch museum to own several major works by Bosch, of which *The Vagabond* is perhaps the most famous. For a long time it was erroneously regarded and titled as a portrait of the Prodigal Son, but the identity of the intriguing pedlar on this panel, rendered entirely in greys and browns, cannot be ascertained. It is thought that he is Alberoyt (literally 'down and out'), an allegorical figure who brought about people's downfall and whose image was seen as a warning to the beholder.

2
Joachim Patenier
(Bouvignes or Dinant *c*1480 – Antwerp 1524)
Landscape with the Burning of Sodom and Gomorrah
Panel, 23 × 29.5 cm
Coll. F. Koenigs, on loan from The Netherlands Office for Fine Arts

3
Hieronymus Bosch
(Bois-le-Duc *c*1450 – Bois-le-Duc 1516)
St Christopher
Panel, 113 × 71.5 cm
Coll. F. Koenigs, 1940; inv. St26
The huge figure of St Christopher, the patron saint of travellers, was highly popular in the Middle Ages. The giant carrying the Infant Jesus on his back is shown in a panoramic landscape full of enigmatic details.

1

2

3

1
Gerard David
(Oudewater *c*1460 – Bruges 1523)
Virgin and Child
Panel, 42.5 × 26 cm
Coll. D. G. van Beuningen 1958;
inv. 2446

2
Adriaen van Wesel
(Utrecht *c*1417 – Utrecht *c*1490)
The Last Supper
Polychrome oak, 52 × 55 cm
Purchased 1940; inv. 1054/St20

3
Jan Gossaert
(Maubeuge *c*1478 – Middelburg 1535)
The Metamorphosis of Hermaphroditus and Salmacis
Panel 32.8 × 21.5 cm
Coll. D. G. van Beuningen 1958;
inv. 2451

In 1523 Margaret of Austria, governess of the Netherlands and resident
in Malines, was given this little
painting by Philip of Burgundy. It
depicts the tale, related in Ovid's
Metamorphoses, of the nymph Salmacis who, in despair because of her
unrequited love for Hermaphroditus, entreats the gods to unite their
bodies for ever. The panel was
painted by Jan Gossaert, who
worked at the court of Philip of Burgundy, the bastard son of Philip the
Good. Gossaert accompanied his
master to Italy in 1503, making him
one of the first artists from the
North to see the remains of Classical
Antiquity. Despite the 'old-
fashioned' look of the delicate,
detailed technique, Gossaert's
choice of subject, his predilection for
nudes and his use of Vitruvian proportion clearly identify him as one
of the early advocates of Renaissance ideals.

1

2

1

1
Lucas van Leyden
(Leyden 1489 – Leyden 1533)
Potiphar's Wife shows her Husband
Joseph's Garment, c1512
Panel, 25 × 34.5 cm
Coll. D. G. van Beuningen 1958;
inv. 2455

2
Jan van Scorel
(Schoorl 1495 – Utrecht 1562)
Portrait of a Young Scholar, 1531
Panel, 46.6 × 35 cm
Purchased 1864; inv. 1797
Clad in a doublet, a red cap on his
blond head, this schoolboy who,
according to the inscription, is
twelve years old, looks at us with an
alert expression. In one hand he
holds a goose-quill, in the other a
letter, the contents of which show
through the paper in mirror-image:
'Omnia dat Dominus, non habet
ergo minus (the Lord gives all, but
has no less because of it)'. Such
sententiae taught sixteenth-century
schoolboys not only Latin but
edifying adages. The same function
is served by the text on the balustrade, which reads: 'Who is rich? He
who desires nothing. Who is poor?
The miser.' The saying is of classical
origin, and occurs in an anthology
specially selected by Erasmus for
pupils of the Latin school.

2

26

3

Pieter Bruegel the Elder
(**Breda** (?) *c1525* – **Brussels** 1569)
The Tower of Babel
Panel, 60 × 74.5 cm
Coll. D. G. van Beuningen 1958;
inv. 2443

The theme of the Tower of Babel is based on a passage from the Old Testament (Genesis 11:1–9), and was seen as an example of pride going before a fall. Bruegel's unfinished tower soars up into the clouds, its monumental aspect enhanced by the aerial perspective. The circular ground plan and numerous open arches were inspired by the Roman Colosseum, an edifice which Bruegel very likely saw on his Italian trip of 1553. The ten-storey structure is a hive of activity. Bruegel provides us with a detailed picture of how sixteenth-century builders went about their work. The harbour bears a close resemblance to Antwerp, a prosperous port during that period. Bruegel painted another picture on the same theme, which is in the Kunsthistorisches Museum in Vienna.

1

Karel van Mander
(Meulebeke 1548 – Amsterdam
1606)
The Crossing of the Jordan, 1605
Panel, 106 × 184.5cm
Purchased 1989; inv. 3200

2

Pieter Aertsen
(Amsterdam (?) 1508/9 –
Amsterdam 1575)
The Pancake Baker, 1560
Panel, 86 × 170 cm
Acquired with the aid of the J. P. van
der Schilden Bequest and the Citi-
zens of Rotterdam 1926; inv. 1006

1

2

3
Hendrick Goltzius
(Mühlbracht 1558 – Haarlem 1617)
Portrait of Jan Govertsz van der Aar,
1603
Canvas, 107.5 × 82.7 cm
On loan from coll. P. de Boer,
Amsterdam; inv. Br.P1

3

I

2

5

1
Titian
(Pieve di Cadore c1485/90 –
Venice 1576)
Boy with Dogs in a Landscape
Canvas, 99.5 × 117 cm
Coll. D. G. van Beuningen 1958;
inv. 2569

2
Guercino
(Cento 1591 – Bologna 1666)
Landscape with Bathing Women
Canvas, 36 × 53 cm
Vitale Bloch Bequest 1976; inv. 2900

Italian Bronzes
The museum's collection of Italian
bronzes is the second largest in the
Netherlands. The majority of the
approximately 60 exhibits come
from D. G. van Beuningen's
collection; others are on long loan
from the J. W. Frederiks collection.
Frederiks, the director of an
insurance institute in The Hague,
not only collected objects of
decorative art but also assembled,
with the same feeling for quality, a
splendid collection of bronzes in the
1930s. The small pieces illustrated
here are among the oldest items. All
come from Italy, the cradle of
bronze sculpture. Inspired by
Antique Roman examples,
Florentine artists began to make
small bronze sculptures around 1450.
A little later Padua and the Venetian
area became important production
centres. Nudes, often representing
mythological figures, featured
prominently. At first these
Renaissance bronzes, some of which
served as oil-lamps, ink-wells or
door-knockers, were produced for
the purpose of interior decoration.
In the course of the sixteenth
century they found their way into
art collections and stimulated the
demand for collectors' items.

3
Adriano Fiorentino
(active Florence end of 15th
century)
Hercules, c1480/90
Bronze, height 36.8 cm
On loan from coll.
Mr J. W. Frederiks; inv. LI

4
Padua (first quarter of 16th
century)
Long-Haired Ram
Bronze, height 16.9 cm
On loan from coll.
Mr J. W. Frederiks; inv. LI4

5
Giovanni da Bologna
(Douai 1529 – Florence 1608)
Sleeping Nymph with Satyr
Bronze, height 19.3 cm
Coll. D. G. van Beuningen 1958;
inv. 1123

1

2

3

Peter Paul Rubens
(Siegen 1577 – Antwerp 1640)
The Timber Wagon, after *c*1630
Panel, 49.5 × 54.7 cm
Coll. D. G. van Beuningen 1958;
inv. 2514

Peter Paul Rubens
(Siegen 1577 – Antwerp 1640)
Nereid and Triton
Panel, 14.5 × 14 cm
Coll. F. Koenigs 1940; inv. St32
Rubens' twenty-one oil sketches
form a unique aspect of the Old
Master collection. Whereas the definitive works were often painted by
Rubens' assistants, these preparatory
panels for altarpieces, tapestries or
murals were always the master's
own work. As well as six sketches for
a series of tapestries depicting the
life of Achilles, the museum owns a
number of oil sketches dating from
1636-37 which were intended as
designs for the decoration of the
Torre de la Parada, Philip IV's hunting lodge on the outskirts of Madrid.
One of them is the fluent, vivid
rendering of a Nereid and Triton.

Adriaen Brouwer
(Oudenaerde 1605/06 – Antwerp
1638)
Man in a Tall Hat
Panel, 19.5 × 12 cm
Coll. D. G. van Beuningen 1958;
inv. 2485

Anthony van Dyck
(Antwerp 1599 – London 1641)
St Jerome
Canvas, 165 × 130 cm
Willem van der Vorm Foundation;
inv. VDV22

4

1

2

34

1 Willem Buytewech
(Rotterdam 1591/92 – Rotterdam
1624)
Merry Company
Canvas, 49.3 × 68 cm
Gift of A. C. Mees 1919; inv. 1103

2 Dirck van Delen
(Heusden 1604/05 – Arnemuiden
1671)
Tulip in a Kendi, 1637
Panel, 38.5 × 29 cm
Vitale Bloch Bequest 1976; inv. 2887

3 Frans Hals
(Antwerp c1580 – Haarlem 1666)
Portrait of an Old Lady, 1639
Panel, 29.5 × 21 cm
Coll. D. G. van Beuningen 1958;
inv. 2498

4 Willem Claesz Heda
(Haarlem 1594 – Haarlem 1670)
Still Life with a Silver Tazza, 1634
Panel, 43 × 57 cm
Purchased 1883; inv. 1286

3

4

1

1

Hercules Segers
(Haarlem (?) 1589/90 – The Hague
(?) in or before 1633)
River Valley with Houses
Canvas, 70 × 86.6 cm
Coll. D. G. van Beuningen 1958;
inv. 2525
Hercules Segers' fantastic landscapes
occupy an exceptional place in
Dutch landscape painting. Although
his etchings and paintings were
much sought after in the seventeenth century by Rembrandt and
others, little of his work has sur-

vived; this landscape is one of eleven
extant paintings. A striking element
in the cosmic scene is a small group
of red-roofed houses with stepped
gables. The same houses recur in an
etching by Segers showing the view
from his house on Lindengracht in
Amsterdam. Like his etching technique, Segers' painting is complex
and unconventional. The small,
round dabs of colour in the vegetation form a contrast to the painstak-
ingly accurate rendering of the
houses and the mountains with their
fanciful shapes.

2

Pieter Saenredam
(Assendelft 1597 – Haarlem 1665)
St Mary's Square and St Mary's
Church, Utrecht, 1663
Panel, 110.5 × 139 cm
Purchased 1872; inv. 1765
St Mary's Square in Utrecht is one
of the few exteriors among Pieter
Saenredam's studies of churches.
With its delicate colouring and per-
fect tranquillity, this large painting
ranks as one of his best and most
ambitious works. In the right fore-
ground we see St Mary's Church

(Mariakerk), built in the twelfth
century and pulled down in the
nineteenth. The towers of the
Cathedral and the Buurkerk can be
made out in the background. The
painting is based on a drawing done
on the spot 28 years earlier, when
Saenredam was in Utrecht in 1636.
Saenredam often employed the
squaring or graticulation method to
transfer a construction drawing to
the panel. On this painting the pat-
tern of squares here and there shows
through the thinly applied paint.

1

1
Rembrandt Harmensz van Rijn
(Leyden 1606 – Amsterdam 1669)
The Concord of the State, c1641
Panel, 74.6 × 101 cm
Purchased 1865; inv. 1717

2
Carel Fabritius
(Midden-Beemster 1622 – Delft
1654)
Self Portrait
Panel, 65 × 49 cm
F.J.O. Boijmans Bequest 1847;
inv. 1205

2

3

3
**Rembrandt Harmensz van Rijn
(Leyden 1606 – Amsterdam 1669)**
Titus at his Desk, 1655
Canvas, 77 × 63 cm
Gift to the Museum Boymans by
the Rembrandt Foundation and
120 Friends of the Museum 1940;
inv. St.2
This portrait, an impressive example
of Rembrandt's painting in the 1650s,
was acquired in the early 1940s with
the support of '120 Friends of the
Museum'. An arresting element of

the composition is the front of the
book-rest with its warm reddish-
brown tints. The light glances off the
boy's hands and face, drawing our
attention to his brooding gaze.
Indeed, this moment of silent contemplation seems to be the real subject of the painting. The boy is
probably Rembrandt's son Titus,
who lived from 1641 to 1668. It is not
certain whether Rembrandt
intended to portray his son, or
whether the boy was standing as
model for St John writing the gospel.

1

1
Jacob van Ruisdael
**(Haarlem 1628/29 – Amsterdam
1682)**
The Cornfield
Canvas, 61 × 71 cm
F. J. O. Boijmans Bequest 1847;
inv. 1742

2
Gerard Ter Borch
(Zwolle 1617 – Deventer 1681)
A Lady Spinning
Panel, 34.5 × 27.5 cm
Willem van der Vorm Foundation;
inv. VDV4

3
Gerard Dou
(Leyden 1613 – Leyden 1675)
Lady at her Toilette, 1667
Panel, 75.5 × 58 cm
Gift of Sir Henry Deterding 1936;
inv. 1186

2

4

3

4
Jan Steen
(Leyden 1625/26 – Leyden 1679)
'Easy come, easy go', 1661
Canvas, 79 × 104 cm
Coll. D. G. van Beuningen 1958;
inv. 2527
The inscription on the chimney-
piece enables us to establish the
original title of this painting, a rare
circumstance in seventeenth-
century art. The plaque, flanked by
putti, bears the text 'Easy come, easy
go', a saying which the grinning man
at the table is putting into practice.
Indulging in oysters, he has his eye
not only on the wine but also on the
pretty girl who is offering him a
glass. Perhaps he has been lucky at
tric-trac, the game of chance being
played by two men in the adjacent
room. Good luck can change to bad,
however, a sentiment endorsed by
the painting on the chimney-piece
showing Fortune on a die, with the
sea in the background: one ship is
flying before the wind, another is
sinking in the wild billows.

1

2

3

1
Jan van de Cappelle
(Amsterdam 1625/26 – Amsterdam
1679)
Calm Sea with Sailing Boats
Canvas, 111 × 144 cm
Acquired 1939; inv. St5

2
Aelbert Cuyp
(Dordrecht 1620 – Dordrecht 1691)
Dapple-Grey in a Landscape
Canvas, 91 × 117 cm
Willem van der Vorm Foundation;
inv. VDVII

3
Bartholomeus van der Helst
(Haarlem 1613 (?) – Amsterdam
1670)
*Portrait of Abraham del Court and
Maria de Keerssegieter*, 1654
Canvas, 172 × 146.5 cm
Purchased 1866; inv. 1296
Although this double portrait of
Abraham del Court and Maria de
Keerssegieter was painted three
years after their nuptials, it is
fraught with marriage symbolism.
The intimate gesture with which the
Amsterdam cloth merchant is clasp-
ing his young wife's wrist is both lit-
erally and metaphorically the focal

point of the painting. The gushing
fountain behind the couple is a reference to the garden of love. The
rose which Maria de Keerssegieter is
holding by its stem is a traditional
amatory symbol. The garments are
superbly painted, particularly
Maria's fashionable satin dress with
its silvery white gleam. Van der
Helst was a consummate master of
such effects, a talent which made
him one of the most sought-after
portraitists of his day. Indeed, until
the beginning of the nineteenth century his popularity exceeded that of
Rembrandt and Frans Hals.

1

Giuseppe Recco
(**Naples 1634 – Alicante 1695**)
Still Life with Masks, Books and Musical Instruments
Canvas, 103.5 × 157 cm
Purchased 1963; inv. 2657

2

Mattia Preti
(**Taverna 1613 – Malta 1699**)
Belisarius Receiving Alms
Canvas, 152.5 × 198.5 cm
Purchased with the aid of the Rembrandt Foundation 1991; inv. 3245

The historical figure of Belisarius (*c505-565*), who as a general in the army of the Byzantine emperor Justinian I attempted to win back Italy from the Visigoths, inspired several legends in the fourteenth and fifteenth centuries. According to one of them the warrior fell into disfavour towards the end of his life, finishing up as a blind beggar, a tragic circumstance which is the subject of Mattia Preti's monumental history piece. Preti, who came from southern Italy, portrays the

figures in a dynamic style with pronounced chiaroscuro effects: on the right the blind Belisarius is accepting an obol, a Greek coin, from the hands of a young nobleman. Although the theme occurs a number of times in literature, very few examples are known in art: it is quite possible that Jacques-Louis David, who painted the subject in 1781, derived it from Preti's painting, which was in a French collection at the time.

3

Simon Vouet
(**Paris 1590 – Paris 1647**)
The Virgin Mary Adoring the Christ Child
Canvas, 119 × 132 cm
Purchased 1988; inv. 3171

2

3

45

1

1

Jean Baptiste Chardin
(**Paris 1699 – Paris 1779**)
Grace Before the Meal, 1761
Canvas, 50.5 × 66.5 cm
Coll. D. G. van Beuningen 1958;
inv. 2574

2

Claude Michel, named Clodion
(**Nancy 1738 – Paris 1814**)
Faun and Nymph
Terracotta, height 49 cm
Coll. D. G. van Beuningen 1958;
inv. 1107

3

Roland Delaporte
(**Paris c1724 – Paris 1793**)
Still Life with Fruit and Bread
Canvas, 44.4 × 62.2 cm
Gift of D. G. van Beuningen 1916;
inv. 1121

4

Honoré Daumier
(**Marseille 1808 – Valmondois 1879**)
The Amateurs
Panel, 23.5 × 21 cm
Coll. D. G. van Beuningen 1958;
inv. 2597

2

3

Although the landscapes of the
Barbizon School of painters were
assured of the interest of Dutch collectors in the nineteenth and early
twentieth centuries, these collectors
preferred the Dutch School when it
came to earlier art. D. G. van Beuningen was one of the few to evince
an interest in what was available
beyond the borders of his own country. The first picture he presented to
the museum in 1916 was a French
still life formerly attributed to Chardin but now regarded as the work of
Delaporte. In this superb little painting, a loaf of bread, a jar covered
with a piece of paper and a basket of
fruit are depicted with vigour and
clarity on a stone ledge. Van Beuningen's first acquisition of French art
was followed by many more. It is
thanks to him that the collection
boasts paintings by Chardin, Watteau, Hubert Robert, Pater, Lancret
and Boucher, as well as Clodion's
terracotta faun and nymph, a group
from the collection which formerly
belonged to Catherine II, Czarina of
Russia. In recent years this nucleus
has been increased in the form of
various bequests and purchases,
including a landscape by Claude
Lorrain and an early painting by
Simon Vouet.

4

Department of Prints

Johan Catharinus Justus Bierens de Haan (1867-1951)
In order to impress the fragility of his collection on people who handle a print or drawing with the arrogance of a politician grasping a newspaper, Dr J. C. J. Bierens de Haan chose a germane passage from Goethe's *Elective Affinities* as the motto on one of his boxes of prints. Even so, the physician and art connoisseur was not a man to keep his collection to himself. All the time he was assembling it, he was envisaging its ultimate home in the Boymans Museum.

Bierens de Haan, the youngest of nine children, was born in 1867 in Leyden, where his father was a professor of mathematics. On leaving grammar school he decided to study medicine; it was during this period that he developed his love of prints. Summer vacations were spent in various European cities, sojourns which not only benefited his medical studies but also gave him a chance to visit the print rooms.

A man of great erudition and wide reading, Bierens de Haan was anything but a scholarly recluse. When the second Boer War broke out in 1899 the doctor manned the ambulances sent by the Dutch Red Cross to the Transvaal and the Orange Free State. In 1912 he set off for another theatre of war to be an eye-witness of the Balkan conflict in Greece. In March 1913 King George I of Greece, with whom Bierens de Haan was on friendly terms, died from injuries sustained from an attempt on his life at Saloniki, breathing his last on the doctor's camp bed. Bierens de Haan volunteered his services yet again in World War I and ran the Dutch hospital in the Bois de Boulogne on the outskirts of Paris. In between these lengthy sojourns abroad he worked as a surgeon at the Eudokia infirmary in Rotterdam, where he also set up a training course for nurses and midwives.

Although Bierens de Haan assembled some 800 examples of graphic art during these years, including a large number of contemporary prints, he did not seriously embark on his collection until later. In 1919 he retired from medicine and in 1923, following a period of extensive foreign travel, he settled in Amsterdam, where he devoted himself exclusively to building up his collection of old prints.

Bierens de Haan probably decided quite early that the Boymans Museum was to have his collection, inspired perhaps by the example of A. J. Domela Nieuwenhuis, who presented his collection of drawings and prints to the museum in 1923. This gift was an important impulse to the print room, which up to then had not been noted for its size or quality. In view of Domela Nieuwenhuis's concentration on such great masters as Dürer, Rembrandt and Goya – whose best impressions, incidentally, he did not always manage to procure – Bierens de Haan decided to avoid duplication and focus on minor, more affordable artists. Aided by his profound knowledge and an innate sense of quality, he assembled a collection of great richness in the years that followed, which boasts work not only by such great artists as Goltzius and Bruegel but also brilliant examples of hitherto undiscovered masters. Highlights are sixteenth-century Dutch and Flemish prints, a series of superb landscapes by seventeenth-century artists, and the virtually complete collection of Adriaen van Ostade's prints. Like van Beuningen, Koenigs and many others, Bierens de Haan obtained a number of important works of art from old royal collections which the German recession forced on to the market. The acquisition of extremely rare prints from the large and celebrated collection of King Frederik Augustus II of Saxony (1797-1854) is just one example.

At the time of his death in December 1951 Bierens de Haan owned some 26,000 prints. He left not only this magnificent collection to the museum but also a sum of money, the annual interest on which was earmarked for additions to the collection. Known as the Lucas van Leyden Fund, this money has enabled numerous purchases to be made, not only in the already well-represented area of prints from the sixteenth and seventeenth centuries but also nineteenth-century specimens. Today, the museum's collection of prints, with approximately 150,000 sheets, is one of the most important of its kind.

Department of Drawings

Franz Koenigs (1881-1941)

'Koenigs had the taste of a true collector: he wanted simply everything,' an art dealer once said. Indeed, the German banker was driven by the passion to collect: in a mere ten years he built up a collection of old drawings comparable in quality with collections formed over hundreds of years. Franz Koenigs was born in 1881 in Kierberg, near Cologne, into a wealthy German family of bankers and textile manufacturers. The boy went into banking, succeeding his uncle Felix as director of the bank Delbrück, Schickler & Cie in 1913, having broken off his law studies and successfully concluded a business deal in Romania. That same year he married Anna, daughter of the German painter Leopold von Kalckreuth who shared his passionate love of art.

Koenigs started off by buying a few paintings, one of which was *St Christopher* by Hieronymus Bosch, but from 1922 he concentrated on old master drawings. This change of direction coincided with his move to the Netherlands, where he settled in Haarlem and entered into a partnership with a Belgian cousin to set up the Rhodius-Koenigs Trading Company. He could not have chosen a better moment to do so; on 11 January 1923 the French occupied the Ruhr region and the German mark was catastrophically devalued. The credit business flourished, partly due to German industry's urgent need for hard currency because of inflation. In the course of his frequent business trips Koenigs took every opportunity to swell his collection. It gradually assumed almost encyclopedic proportions, providing a survey which ranged from the late Middle Ages up to and including the nineteenth century.

Koenigs relied on his astonishing perspicacity and universal taste. The times favoured him, too: the economic crisis was forcing many people to sell their collections, often formed in the course of centuries. Among the treasures thus procured by Koenigs were two albums containing more than 100 drawings by Fra Bartolommeo, from the collection of the Duke of Saxe-Weimar; he even managed to make good a lost opportunity by obtaining the desirable items acquired six years earlier by Julius W. Böhler, a Swiss collector who was now compelled to sell. With close on 1,000 drawings of the Italian School, 300 German drawings, more than 500 French sheets from the seventeenth, eighteenth and nineteenth centuries and 700 seventeenth-century Dutch drawings, Koenigs built up a fabulous collection in an astonishingly short space of time.

In the early 1930s, however, the tide turned even for Koenigs, and he was obliged to take out a loan with the Lisser & Rosencranz bank, with the collection as collateral. Lisser & Rosencranz allowed him to house it in the Boymans Museum which, under Hannema's directorship, had not only recently moved into a new building but was also establishing a reputation for important exhibitions.

The danger of impending war had its effect on Koenigs' collection. In 1939, due to the Jewish bank's decision to relocate in America, the irreplaceable collection was in danger of being sold abroad. Hannema endeavoured to persuade the industrialists van der Vorm and van Beuningen, who had frequently demonstrated their allegiance to the museum during this period, to enable the collection to remain.

In the end van Beuningen himself bought the drawings in 1940 and at the end of that year presented them to the museum foundation. He had, however, had to sell one-fifth of the collection to the German occupiers; the Germans had ordered Posse, director of the Staatliche Gemälde-sammlungen in Dresden, to purchase and confiscate works of art for a new Führer Museum to be built in Linz. Posse made a selection from the French, Dutch, Flemish and Italian schools, but what interested him most were the German drawings, which he bought practically in toto. On 25 May 1941, a few weeks after Koenigs' death in an accident at Cologne railway station, the drawings were taken to the print room in Dresden. When the Dutch government claimed their return after the war under international law, they had disappeared without trace. The search for the 526 missing drawings led in 1987 to the return of 35 German sheets. In the autumn of 1992, 360 of the remaining ones turned up in Russia. It is hoped that these, too, will be returned, so that Franz Koenigs' unique collection, to which the museum's print room rightly owes its fame, can be reunited at last.

Franz Koenigs, photograph, *c*1930

1
Unknown artist (Germany, c1465)
Revelations 20: 4-6
Hand-coloured woodcut,
126 × 196 mm
Gift of Domela Nieuwenhuis
inv. DN69/9
This hand-coloured woodcut from a
block book is one of the earliest
examples of printing, with text and
print carved in a single block. The
Latin text, a passage from the Book
of Revelations, describes the resur-
rection of faithful believers. St John
is depicted alongside the text, ges-
turing towards a large bed on which
the dead are represented by a few
men, women and a child. The small
naked children on the pillow sym-
bolize the souls of the faithful.

2
Juste de Juste (active c1540)
School of Fontainebleau
Athletes
Etching, 266 × 200 mm
Gift of Domela Nieuwenhuis;
inv. OB1557

3
Peter Opel
(active in Regensburg 1580-95)
A plough drawn by sixty horses, 1587
Etching, 192 × 630 mm
Gift of Bierens de Haan;
inv. BdH14625

4
Hendrick Goltzius
(Mühlbracht 1558 – Haarlem 1617)
The nymph Galatea
Chiaroscuro woodcut, 348 × 264 mm
Gift of Bierens de Haan;
inv. BdH2644

1

2

3

4

5

an Muller

Amsterdam 1571 – Amsterdam (628)

The division of dark and light, 1589
Engraving, diameter 262 mm
Purchased 1964; inv. L1964/131 B
This engraving, the second of a series of seven prints, depicts the first day of Creation. An angel with a crossed staff is dividing light and darkness. Day, in the guise of a male nude, is resolutely striding towards the brilliant light, while Night, personified by a female figure, is shrouded in a dark robe strewn with stars. The print was made by Jan Muller from a design by the Haarlem draughtsman and engraver Hendrick Goltzius (1558–1617). During this period Haarlem was the centre in Holland for new ideas about art from Italy. Inspired by Michelangelo and others, the Haarlem mannerists took the idealized nude as their principal theme. Not only in mythological representations but in biblical scenes too, their nudes are posed in attitudes of the utmost artificiality and tension.

51

1

2

3

1
Jan Brosterhuisen
(Leiden 1596 – Breda 1650)
Landscape
Etching, 165 × 235 mm
Gift of Bierens de Haan;
inv. BdH6793

2
Stefano della Bella
(Florence 1610 – Florence 1664)
Boy with two puppies
Etching, 147 × 137 mm
Purchased 1989; inv. L1989/210

3
Giovanni Battista Piranesi
(Mogliano 1720 – Rome 1778)
Hadrian's Villa, the Canopus, 1768
Etching, 444 × 577 mm
Gift of Bierens de Haan; inv. BdH133
Piranesi made ten etchings of

Hadrian's Villa, the sumptuous imperial residence built at Tivoli, near Rome, in 118 AD. They belong to his *Vedute di Roma*, 135 views of the city, 130 of which are in the museum's possession. Piranesi did more than just register what he saw. The architecture of the ruin, overgrown with lush vegetation, is rendered here in a dramatic chiaroscuro. The dwarfed figures accentuate the scale of this impressive *exedra*, which Hadrian built to commemorate the city of Canopus in Egypt.

4
Pierre Bonnard
(Fontenay-aux-Roses 1867 – Le Cannet 1947)
La Petite Blanchisseuse, 1896
Lithograph, 293 × 195 mm
Purchased 1953; inv. MB1953/75

5
Pablo Picasso
(Malaga 1881 – Antibes 1973)
Still life beside the sea, 1929
Colour etching, 371 × 268 mm
Purchased 1929; inv. OB1600
Picasso's etching of this still life is based on a gouache which he had painted at St Raphael ten years earlier, in the summer of 1919. In this colour etching the artist contrasts the tradition of illusionism and the cubist idiom which he and Braque had developed. Perspective and shadow effects are back again, and monochromy has given way to brilliant colours. The guitar, that indispensable attribute of cubist still lifes, is still there. The instrument evidently held considerable charm for Picasso, not only as a reminder of his Spanish origins but also for its formal potential.

4

5

1

2

3

This sheet is thought to be one of
the few absolutely authentic drawings by Hieronymus Bosch. The
painstaking rendering suggests that
this is a work in its own right and
not a preparatory study. The principal motif of an owl is quite common
in Bosch's work; it probably symbolizes sin and evil, which shun the
light of day. The gallows in the
background might be a warning
against vice and sinfulness. The
composition, with the owl featured
prominently in the middle, has a
rather modern look, and has
occasionally prompted comparisons
with a film close-up. It is more
likely, however, that the drawing has
been cropped all round, making it
even harder to interpret Bosch's
work, which is always difficult to
fathom.

The period in which Andrea Vendramin governed Venice and the
date of Bellini's sojourn in that city
enable this drawing to be dated
1476/78. The Venetian doge, wearing
a *corno* on his head, posed for this
portrait in the company of the papal
nuncio. Behind Vendramin, slightly
to one side, is his secretary. The
brocade cloth hanging from the
balustrade displays the family arms.
The official character of the portrait
is enhanced by the materials – the
work is painted on costly vellum and
there is gold leaf in the brocade on
the balustrade.

4

1

Albrecht Dürer
(Nuremberg 1471 – Nuremberg 1528)
The Holy Family.
Gouache, heightened with gold, on
vellum, 170 × 116 mm
On loan from the Netherlands Office
for Fine Arts; inv. MB1987/T30

2

Albrecht Dürer
(Nuremberg 1471 – Nuremberg 1528)
Study of two feet
Brush and grey ink, grey wash,
heightened with white, on green
prepared paper, 176 × 216 mm
Coll. D. G. van Beuningen 1958;
inv. MB1958/T24
At the beginning of 1507 Albrecht
Dürer was commissioned by Jacob
Heller, a Frankfurt merchant, to
paint an altarpiece on the theme of
the Assumption. The Heller Altar
became so famous that in 1614 the
central panel was taken from the
Dominican monastery in Frankfurt
to become the property of Maxi-
milian, Elector of Bavaria. Unfortu-
nately it was destroyed in a fire in
the Electoral residence in Munich in
1729. Besides a seventeenth-century
copy, a series of superb studies by
Dürer immortalize the celebrated
triptych. One of these preliminary
drawings is of a pair of feet,
executed in grey ink on coloured
paper and skilfully heightened in
white.

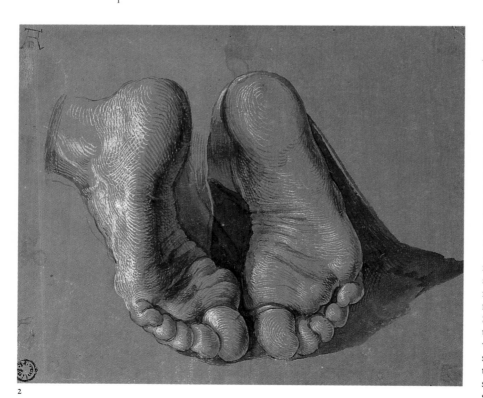

2

3

Pieter Bruegel the Elder
(Breda (?) c1525 – Brussels 1569)
Fortitudo
Pen and brown ink, 225 × 295 mm
Coll. F. Koenigs 1940; inv. N189
In 1559-60, at the request of the
Antwerp publisher of prints Hieronymus Cock, Pieter Bruegel drew
designs for a series of prints
depicting the seven cardinal virtues,
including this representation of Fortitude. Bruegel bore the purpose of
these drawings in mind while engaged on them, executing the hatching
with the utmost accuracy in order to
simplify the engraver's task. The
representation is rife with symbolism. The fortress in the background
represents faith. From it, knights
attack the powers of evil, which are
rendered in a manner reminiscent of
figures by Hieronymus Bosch.
Standing in the midst of the fray is
the personification of Fortitude: her
wings of victory spread out wide,
she tramples on a dragon. Each of
the animals being killed around her
symbolizes one of the seven deadly
sins.

4
**Jan van der Straet, called
Stradanus
(Bruges 1523 – Florence 1605)**
Odysseus in the cave

Pen and brown ink, blue and white
wash, heightened with white,
182 × 270 mm
F. J. O. Boijmans Bequest 1847;
inv. J. Stradanus 212

3

4

1

Cosimo Tura
(**Ferrara c1430 – Ferrara 1495**)
Hercules and the Nemean Lion
Pen and wash, heightened with
white, 210 × 150 mm
Coll. F. Koenigs 1940; inv. I 180

2

Fra Bartolommeo
(**Florence 1472 – Florence 1517**)
Study of a standing man
Red chalk, 287 × 197 mm
Coll. F. Koenigs 1940; inv. 1563M3
The museum is unique in owning
more than five hundred preparatory
drawings by Fra Bartolommeo. Until
quite recently the sheets were kept
between the two red morocco covers
in which Cavaliere Gabburi had had
them bound more than 250 years
ago. In 1727 Gabburi, a Florentine
collector, had discovered the drawings in a convent in Florence. Their
presence there was due to Fra Pao-
lino, Bartolommeo's favourite pupil,
who kept them as a stockpile of
motifs after his teacher's death and
gave them to Sister Plautilla in
about 1550. Fra Bartolommeo drew
this study in red chalk in preparation for a large altarpiece with the
Madonna della Misericordia, now in
the Pinacoteca at Lucca. The
models portrayed in the drawing
occur on the altarpiece in the group
of supplicants sheltering under the
Virgin's cloak.

3

Federico Barocci
(**Urbino 1535 – Urbino 1612**)
Study for a dead Christ
Black and white chalk, 257 × 373 mm
Coll. F. Koenigs 1940; inv. I 428

4

Jacopo Carucci, called Pontormo
(**Pontormo 1494 – Florence 1557**)
Two seated youths
Red chalk, 277 × 379 mm
Coll. F. Koenigs 1940; inv. I 117

2

3

4

1

Hendrick Goltzius
(Mühlbracht 1558 – Haarlem 1617)
Sight
Pen and brown ink, with wash,
heightened with white, 160 × 124 mm
F. J. O. Boijmans Bequest 1847;
inv. H. Goltzius 4
The museum owns four Goltzius
drawings which served as designs for
a series of engravings of the Five
Senses. Each sense is symbolized by
a loving couple accompanied by an
animal in which the sense in ques-
tion is particularly well developed.
In *Sight* an elderly man is making
bold advances to an elegant lady. He
is holding up a mirror to her, an
attribute which, like the cat on the
right, is a highly apt reference to the
subject. Goltzius seems to have put
two meanings into these drawings:
whereas the tender music-making
couple in *Hearing* exemplify har-
monious love, the drawing reproduced here would appear to
underline a negative amatory aspect.

2

Pieter Saenredam
(Assendelft 1597 – Haarlem 1665)
Interior of St Janskerk in Utrecht
Black and white chalk, pen and
brown ink, heightened with white,
on blue paper, 277 × 414 mm
Coll. F. Koenigs 1940; inv. H183

3

Aelbert Cuyp
(Dordrecht 1620 – Dordrecht 1691)
View of Scheveningen
Black chalk, brush in grey and
watercolour, 185 × 480 mm
Coll. F. Koenigs 1940; inv. H70

1

2

4

Cornelis Dusart
(Haarlem 1660 – Haarlem 1704)
A seated man
Black and red chalk, 310 × 210 mm
F. J. O. Boijmans Bequest 1847;
inv. MB338
The majority of the drawings from
the F. J. O. Boijmans Bequest were
destroyed by a fire in the museum in
1864; this carefully worked-up red
and black chalk drawing is one of
the few sheets to have survived.
Cornelis Dusart was a pupil of
Adriaen van Ostade, and portrayed
his male model in several drawings
from different angles. Dusart obvi-
ously paid great attention to detail,
lavishing extra care on the fabrics.
This particular skill is certainly one
reason why his drawings were much
sought after as works of art in their
own right.

4

1

1
Rembrandt Harmensz van Rijn
(Leyden 1606 – Amsterdam 1669)
Saskia at a window
Pen and brown ink, with wash,
236 × 178 mm
Coll. F. Koenigs 1940; inv. R131

2
Rembrandt Harmensz van Rijn
(Leyden 1606 – Amsterdam 1669)
View of Diemen
Pen and brown ink, with wash,
105 × 184 mm
Coll. D. G. van Beuningen 1958; inv.
MB1958/T22

3
Rembrandt Harmensz van Rijn
(Leyden 1606 – Amsterdam 1669)
Study of a Syndic
Pen and brush in brown ink, brown
wash, corrected and heightened with
white, 225 × 175 mm
Coll. F. Koenigs 1940; inv. R133

2

3

Rembrandt was a prolific draughts-man who employed the medium not merely in order to study various physical attitudes or as a direct preparation for his paintings, but just as much to capture fleeting moments in daily life or the surrounding countryside. Although the Rot-terdam collection of Rembrandt drawings is not as extensive as those in Berlin, London and Amsterdam, more than thirty sheets provide a virtually complete survey of his many-faceted draughtsmanship. One of the highlights is the drawing of Saskia, Rembrandt's wife against the background of a dim interior, audaciously rendered in heavy washes. Leaning on the window-sill, she seems to be trying to catch the beholder's eye. The impressive study for one of the 'Syndics', the famous group portrait of cloth inspectors which Rembrandt painted in 1662, is drawn on paper from a ledger. He seems to have experi-mented at such length with the pos-ition of the left hand and the broad-rimmed hat that the paper has suf-fered a certain amount of wear and tear. The view shows Rembrandt's skill in depicting the landscape; a winding country road in the other-wise empty foreground leads the eye towards the village, which is evoked in a few lines and subtle washes.

I

Peter Paul Rubens
(Siegen 1577 – Antwerp 1640)
Young woman with folded hands
Red and black chalk, heightened
with white, 473 × 354 mm
Coll. F. Koenigs 1940; inv. V81

Anthony van Dyck
(Antwerp 1599 – London 1641)
Crucifixion
Pen and brown ink, brown wash
over black chalk, corrected with
white, 300 × 253 mm
Coll. D. G. van Beuningen 1958;
inv. MB1958/T25

Jacob Jordaens
(Antwerp 1593 – Antwerp 1678)
The king drinking
Black chalk and body colour,
heightened with white,
504 × 650 mm
Coll. F. Koenigs 1940; inv. V91
This detailed drawing probably
served as a model for Jordaens' assistants when painting his pictures.
The subject is Twelfth Night, a
theme frequently depicted by Jordaens. Young and old are indulging in
food and drink, singing loudly. Jordaens' father-in-law, the painter
Adam van Noort, was probably the
model for the old man sitting in the
centre of the picture. The crown on
his head shows that he is the lucky
finder of the bean baked into the
cake traditionally eaten on Twelfth
Night; his reward is to be king for a
day. The bagpipe player with his
distended cheeks and his instrument's taut windbag is a familiar
figure in Jordaens' paintings, occur-
ring in a similar representation of
the Flemish saying 'Soo d'oude
songen, soo pepen de ionge (as the
old sang, so the young cheeped)'.

2

3

1

2

1

Herman Henstenburgh
(Hoorn 1667 – Hoorn 1726)
Nine exotic insects
Watercolour and body colour on
vellum, 231 × 342 mm
Purchased in 1866; inv. MB339
Herman Henstenburgh was not only
a pastrycook but a highly proficient
draughtsman. His deceptively life-
like renderings of all manner of
insects were painted with body
colour on costly vellum. Shadows,
added in wash, raise the vividly
coloured creatures to their feet,
cleverly bringing them to life.
According to his biographer, Johan
van Gool, Henstenburgh experi-
mented with pigments, achieving an
intensity and clarity which rivalled
oils in several ways. However, van
Gool goes on to tell us that the
artist, 'for all his talent, was wasted
in his native town of Hoorn, where
no art-lover of note ever came.'

2
J. A. Brandt
(Amsterdam 1788 – Amsterdam
1821)
A spray of flowers
Watercolour and body colour,
205 × 185 mm
F. J. O. Boijmans Bequest 1847;
inv. A. J. Brandt 1

3
Francesco Guardi
(Venice 1712 – Venice 1793)
Landscape
Pen and brown ink, brown wash,
257 × 388 mm
Coll. F. Koenigs 1940; inv. I 141

4
Giambattista Tiepolo
(Venice 1696 – Madrid 1770)
View from Tiepolo's house in Venice
Pen and brown ink, brown wash on
white prepared paper, 153 × 283 mm
Coll. F. Koenigs 1940; inv. I 217

1

2

3

Jean-Honoré Fragonard
(Grasse 1732 – Paris 1806)
View in a Roman ruin
Red chalk, 264 × 383 mm
Coll. F. Koenigs 1940; inv. FI 162

2
Jean-Antoine Watteau
(Valenciennes 1684 – Nogent-sur-
Marne 1721)
Study sheet with four soldiers and a
standing woman
Red chalk, 188 × 198 mm
Coll. F. Koenigs 1940; inv. FI 150
This drawing comes from the collection of an eighteenth-century collector and amateur, Pierre-Jean
Mariette, and enjoys what connois-
seurs regard as 'a distinguished
provenance'; in the bottom right-
hand corner is Mariette's collector's
mark. Watteau, a great favourite of
Mariette, drew innumerable such
figure studies, choosing as his
models members of the *beau monde*,
characteristic street folk or beggars.
His drawings are often overcrowded;
the existence of numerous sheets
bearing just one study suggests that
later art dealers made the most of
the artist's *horror vacui*, ruthlessly
attacking many a well-filled sheet
with the scissors.

3
Jean-Antoine Watteau
(Valenciennes 1684 – Nogent-sur-
Marne 1721)
Man standing with outstretched arm
Red, black and white chalk,
272 × 189 mm
Coll. F. Koenigs 1940; inv. FI 281

4
Jean-Auguste-Dominique Ingres
(Montauban 1780 – Paris 1867)
Portrait of Mme Reiset and her daughter
Pencil, heightened with white,
308 × 245 mm
Coll. F. Koenigs; inv. F II 168

5
Eugène Delacroix
(Charenton-St Maurice 1798 –
Paris 1863)
Faust and Mephistopheles
Brush and brown ink over pencil,
305 × 465 mm
Coll. F. Koenigs 1940; Inv. F II 3
Delacroix was a fervent admirer of
Goethe and illustrated the first part
of the German poet's tragedy, *Faust*.
This drawing is one of the prelimin-
ary studies for a series of seventeen
lithographs published in 1828. It
shows the scene in which Mephis-
topheles and Faust pass by a raised
place of execution called the
Ravenstone on their way to the
dungeon where Faust's beloved

4

5

Gretchen is imprisoned. In a few
telling lines the gallows field where,
according to popular lore, witches
held their sabbaths, is indicated at
the top left of the sheet. Faust stares
up at it aghast, reining in his horse
and trying to restrain his companion
with his left hand. But to no avail:
Mephistopheles rides on, inexorable.

1

1
Edouard Manet
(Paris 1832 – Paris 1883)
Letter with plums, 1880
Pen and watercolour, 202 × 126 mm
Coll. F. Koenigs 1940; inv. F II 72
For reasons of health, Manet, known
as the painter of modern life, spent
the summer of 1880 away from Paris.
From Bellevue he sent a number of
letters embellished with watercolours. This charming token was
probably addressed to Mme Guill-
emet, an American lady who ran a
well-known Paris fashion shop with
her husband. The Guillemets, who a
year previously had posed for
Manet's painting *In the Conservatory*
(now in the Nationalgalerie, Berlin),
were close friends of the artist.
That same year Manet painted a
number of little still lifes which, like
the illustrated letters, were meant
for his friends.

2
Johan Barthold Jongkind
(Lattrop 1819 – La Côte-St-André
1891)
View of the Haringvliet at Rotterdam,
1868
Watercolour over black chalk,
273 × 443 mm
Purchased in 1977; inv. MB1977/T7
In 1849 the painter Jongkind left
Holland for France, which became
his second fatherland. He was a
gifted watercolourist, his outdoor
sketches serving as the basis for oil
paintings executed in the studio.
This lovely view of the Haringvliet
in Rotterdam, painted during a
family visit in 1868, evokes the
atmosphere of a day in late summer
in fluent touches of well-balanced
colour. Thirteen years later
Jongkind used it for a painting now
in the Rijksmuseum, Amsterdam.

3
Paul Cézanne
(Aix-en-Provence 1839 – Aix-en-
Provence 1906)
View of L'Estaque
Watercolour and white body colour
over black chalk, 310 × 475 mm
Coll. F. Koenigs 1940; inv. F II 183

2

3

Department of Applied Art and Design

Elie van Rijckevorsel (1845–1928)

In 1910 the museum was given an important collection of nearly 500 items of glass and porcelain from a donor who wished to remain anonymous. The extremely high quality of the pieces – especially the glass – made the gift particularly welcome, all the more so because it meant a fresh start for the museum's collection of decorative art, which had been almost entirely destroyed by fire in 1864. A large proportion was immediately placed on permanent display in the upper hall of the Schielandshuis which, according to the annual report, 'to the visitor ascending the staircase now [makes] an agreeable, welcoming impression, whereas the former empty [space] was more oppressive.'

Over the next few years the same collector donated more pieces of exceptional quality, including Lady Harvey's Glass, an extremely large early eighteenth-century goblet. Not until the donor's death in 1928, when he bequeathed the rest of his collection to the museum, was his identity revealed as Dr Elie van Rijckevorsel.

A member of a prominent family of Rotterdam merchants, Elie van Rijckevorsel was the youngest of four children born to Huibert van Rijckevorsel, a ship owner. His sister and two brothers died young, leaving him the sole surviving child, at four years old. Elie broke with the family tradition of business: in 1863, a year after his father's death, he started to study higher mathematics and classics in Utrecht; he finally graduated *magna cum laude* in physics in 1872. Fascinated by geomagnetism and its influence on the weather, he undertook research which required considerable travel. On the advice of his professor, the famous meteorologist Buys Ballot, he went to the Dutch East Indies, where he observed geomagnetic phenomena in remote areas between 1873 and 1877. This was followed by two long tours of Brazil between 1880 and 1884. The Brazilian emperor Pedro II placed a government ship at his disposal, enabling him to carry out his research along the coast. He also sailed the Itapicuru and Parahyba rivers in a small craft, accompanied by a single Dutch servant.

As well as scientific data, van Rijckevorsel brought back many impressions of the countries he had visited and their inhabitants, experiences which he published on his return in *Letters from Insulinde* (1878) and *Out of Brazil* (1886). He also brought back numerous ethnographic items, fabrics and weapons, presenting them to Rotterdam's Ethnographic Museum which he was instrumental in founding in 1885.

Despite never holding a paid position, in scientific circles he was held in very high esteem, and in 1896 became a member of the Permanent Commission of the International Meteorological Committee in Paris. Two years later he received an honorary doctorate in Glasgow from Lord Kelvin, the celebrated Scottish physicist.

H. J. Haverman (1857-1928)
Portrait of Mr and Mrs van
Rijckevorsel-Kolff, oil on canvas

From 1886 to 1904 van Rijckevorsel was active in local politics, becoming a Liberal member of the city council. Although his nature and talents were less suited to the role of a politician, he did much for public education in his capacity of education expert on the council, founding an Industrial School for girls and a school for backward children.

Van Rijckevorsel lived in Rotterdam at number 3 Parklaan, a house which the architect van den Brink had built for his mother in 1869–71; he shared it with her until her death in 1893. From 1909 he lived there with his wife Jacoba Elisabeth Kolff, whom he married when he was 64. He impressed his personality on the interior of the house, which survives virtually intact. For the library he had two ornately decorated doors made of ebony which he had brought back from his travels; the woodwork in the various rooms and the tiled compositions above the doors were done to his designs, and he was also responsible for the ceiling painting in the dining room. His artistic aspirations were, however, most apparent in his collection of antique glass.

The gift of his superb collection, and also the Erasmus Foundation which he established in 1911, have been of invaluable benefit to the museum. Van Rijckevorsel put a large portion of his capital into the foundation, which is dedicated to the promotion of science, art and education in Rotterdam; the museum appeals to it when help is needed for the purchase of a costly object of art.

Pre-Industrial Utensils

Hendrik Jan van Beuningen (born 1920)

The collection amassed by Hendrik Jan van Beuningen and his wife Miem de Vriese over a period of 40 years was literally there for the taking. The van Beuningens were the first Dutch collectors of pre-industrial household objects – eating, drinking and cooking vessels, chamber pots, lamps and candlesticks dating from the eleventh to the nineteenth centuries. Commonplace items of this nature, to be found in every home, almost always met with the same fate: having served their purpose for many years they were discarded, vanishing into the soil where they either decayed or resurfaced hundreds of years later.

Although van Beuningen obtained the great majority of his collection of more than 10,000 objects from other people, he was not averse to digging in cesspits and rubbish tips himself in search of buried treasures. As a child he was fascinated by this activity, and spent many a summer in Drenthe, in the east of the country, hunting for prehistorical fragments of urns, arrowheads and scrapers. On the advice of his father he abandoned the idea of becoming an archeologist and went into business. His first position was in the Rotterdam office of the coal trading company where his uncle, D. G. van Beuningen, was in charge. Archeology, however, remained an engrossing pastime.

The Rotterdam bombardment of May 1940 destroyed van Beuningen's growing collection of prehistorical objects but, unexpectedly, it also opened up the way to the present collection. Reconstruction of the city began immediately. Due to the lack of oil and petrol, manpower was used to clear the ground for building. The boggy Rotterdam soil was discovered to have been conducive to the survival of all sorts of remains from different layers of habitation throughout the centuries, and the excavations brought a host of interesting objects to light. Although the museums did their best to acquire these treasures, the labourers sold many finds to antique dealers and private individuals. The core of van Beuningen's collection was formed when a digger threw him a clod of mud, saying 'this is right up your street'. The pewter jug which emerged from the shapeless mass formed the beginning of his new collection. In the years that followed, van Beuningen often stopped off at building sites on his daily bicycle rides to work to swap potato and cigarette coupons and – in very special cases – alcohol coupons for additions to his collection.

At first van Beuningen concentrated on pewter, which was readily available since Rotterdam had been a centre of the pewter industry. In 1955, when the Boymans Museum acquired the Verster pewter collection partly with van Beuningen's help, he presented number of important pieces excavated in Rotterdam. He then concentrated on pottery. In the 1960s many objects were found in the course of large-scale development schemes in old city centres, even though bulldozers reduced the chances of finding undamaged specimens. By this time local governments appreciated the importance of excavations. Van Beuningen was active in setting up the Advisory Coordination Commission for Archeological Research in the Rotterdam area. Amateur archeologists were now joined by professionals on the municipal payroll.

Thanks partly to his contacts with experts, van Beuningen began to form a clearer idea of what he wanted from his collection: to obtain as complete a picture as possible of the development of earthenware from the eleventh century to the nineteenth, when handcraft was superseded by machine production. Besides Dutch earthenware, van Beuningen collected household pottery from neighbouring countries, many items coming from important production centres in the Rhineland – Cologne, Siegburg, Frechen, Aachen, Langerwehe, Andenne and Raeren.

At first his growing collection was housed in a museum-like extension built on to his house by the former owner. In the 1970s he offered it to the city of Rotterdam on condition that it was to be administered by the Boymans-van Beuningen Museum and exhibited in a new wing. The council accepted these terms in 1981, and the collection was transferred on loan to the museum in instalments, the first of which arrived in 1983. The gift took effect in December 1990, a few months prior to the opening of the van Beuningen-de Vriese Pavilion. The basement of the new gallery houses the Public Study Collection of Utensils; on the ground floor attention is drawn to specific aspects of the collection in changing arrangements.

A few years ago Hendrik Jan van Beuningen referred to collecting as a family weakness which, once acquired, is incurable. This is certainly true of himself. Since handing over his possessions to the museum he has embarked on a new collection – late medieval religious and profane insignia found in the Netherlands, a collection which has already grown into one of the largest in Europe.

North Germany, 13th century
Aquamanile
Copper, height 25 cm
On loan from the J. W. Frederiks
collection; inv. KB61
Simple medieval utensils were made
of reddish-brown earthenware,
pewter or wood, but more costly
vessels were often cast in copper or
bronze. The casting technique
developed into a particularly high
art in the Rhineland area and Meuse
valley. This handsome ewer is in the
shape of a lion, an ancient symbol of
power and strength, and a popular
form for aquamaniles. It was filled
through the opening on top of the
animal's head and emptied by pouring the water through the spout in
its mouth. The aquamanile was an
indispensable ecclesiastical attribute
for hand-washing, but it also graced
the tables of the rich. Only a small
number survive, due to the material
from which they were fashioned:
many bronze and copper objects
were melted down.

I

2
North France, 1460-80
Top of a lectern in the shape of an
eagle
Polychrome walnut, height 87.5 cm
Acquired 1950; inv. 1031

3
Flanders, 1350-1450
Bowl with coat of arms
Earthenware, diameter 45 cm
Coll. van Beuningen-de Vriese;
inv. F5332

3A
Detail of bowl (3)

4
Malines, Belgium, 15th century
Jug
Bronze, height 36 cm
On loan from the J. W. Frederiks
collection; inv. KB44

2

3

4

3A

1

Iznik, Turkey, 16th century
Tiled panel
Glazed earthenware, each
c23.5 × 23.5 cm
Coll. Bastert-van Schaardenburg
1941; inv. A3897

2

Valencia, Spain, beginning 16th century
Dish
Maiolica, diameter 44.3 cm
Coll. Bastert-van Schaardenburg
1941; inv. A3749

3

Deruta, Italy
Dish, c1510
Maiolica, diameter 39 cm
Coll. Bastert-van Schaardenburg
1941; inv. A3649

1

4
Deruta, Italy
Albarello, 1501
Maiolica, height 32 cm
Coll. Bastert-van Schaardenburg
1941; inv. A3648

The museum's collection of Spanish and Italian maiolica has an international reputation. Its nucleus was formed by J. N. Bastert (1891-1976) and his wife in the 1920s and 1930s, the collection being moved to the museum in 1940. Bastert did not lose sight of his treasures, however; as curator for the applied arts from 1941 to 1956, he expanded the maiolica collection. A characteristic feature of this type of earthenware is the white ground of opaque tin glaze on which the decoration is painted in one or more colours. The technique, which hailed from the Middle East, was introduced to Spain by the Arabs in the 11th century. The term maiolica

4

3

comes from Italy, where the ware was named after the major export port, Majorca. In the fifteenth and sixteenth centuries numerous production centres sprang up in Italy; the most important were Faenza, Deruta, Gubbio and Urbino. The decorative plates bearing portraits and biblical or mythological scenes display a high degree of artistic and technical finesse. Right from the start these beautifully painted plates were much admired, prompting many of the painters to sign their work. Another distinctive example of Italian maiolica is the brightly painted albarello, or drug jar; the one shown here contained theriaca, an antipyretic remedy.

1

2

3

2A

1
Circle of François Briot, France, 1550-1600
Mars dish
Pewter, diameter 48.8 cm
Acquired 1956; inv. OM298

2
St Porchaire, France, 16th century
Costrel
Earthenware, height 28 cm
On loan from The Netherlands
Office for Fine Arts; inv. B31

3
Zeeland (?), Netherlands
Dresser, c1600
Oak with intarsia, height 174 cm
Acquired 1942; inv. Div.M.23

3A
Detail of dresser (3)

4
Rotterdam, Netherlands
Nautilus cup, 1590
Silver-gilt mount, nautilus shell,
height 30 cm
On loan from The Netherlands
Office for Fine Arts; inv. MBZ185
The discovery of the New World
had a tremendous impact on science
and art. Countless *naturalia* and *arti-
ficialia* found their way into the cabi-
nets of art and rare objects which
were so popular in the sixteenth and
seventeenth centuries. One such
desirable object was the nautilus
shell. The mollusc's rough exterior
was removed to reveal the beautiful
iridescent shell, which was placed in
a silver mount and transformed into
a sumptuous drinking vessel. This
handsome example is decorated
entirely in a marine vein. The shell
is surmounted by Neptune seated on
a dolphin; the female figure on the
front of the shell recalls a ship's fig-
urehead. Fashioned in Rotterdam, it
was presented to the Czar of Russia
by King Christian IV of Denmark in
the early seventeenth century; it
finally returned to Rotterdam after
World War II.

4

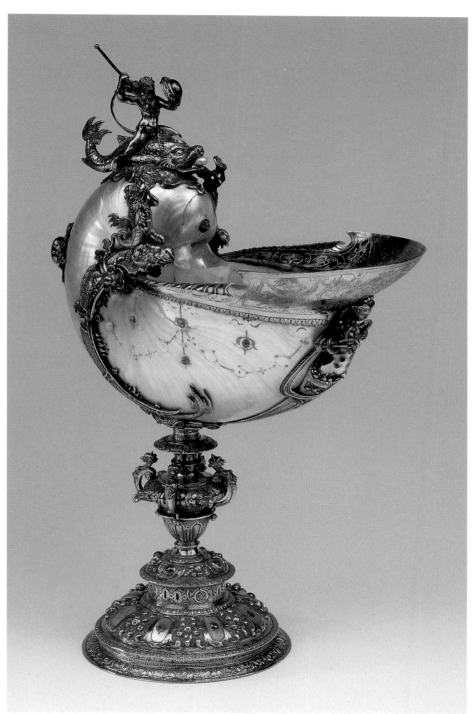

1

2

The seventeenth century was not
only a golden age for Dutch painting
but also a period of consummate
artistic and technical craftsmanship.
The prosperity enjoyed by the
Northern Netherlands as a centre of
world trade was expressed in the
luxurious items with which wealthy
citizens surrounded themselves. The
work of the van Vianen family represented the pinnacle of precious
metalwork. The silver-gilt tazza
decorated with a depiction of Susanna and the Elders is a superb
example; so is the elaborate, sculptural salt-cellar by Adam Vianen's
pupil Michiel de Bruyn, which is
executed in the manner of the
renowned family of Utrecht
silversmiths. There was also a great
demand for decorated drinking
glasses during this period. Marinus
van Gelder's large lidded rummer is
embellished with hunchbacks and
beggars. As was often the case, the
famous glass-engraver took his
motifs from prints, in this instance a
series published in Nancy in 1616 by
Jacques Callot. The small jug topped
with a silver lid, from the Hoppesteyn studio, is illustrative of
attempts to imitate the shapes, colours and decoration of imported
Chinese porcelain. Not until the
eighteenth century did Europeans
find out how to make the substance
themselves; prior to this, Dutch pot-
ters did the best they could (and it
was a pretty good best) by produc-
ing blue delftware.

3

2
Northern Netherlands
Tulip tile picture, *c*1640
Maiolica, 26.8 × 64 cm (total)
Acquired 1958; inv. A5030

Paulus van Vianen,
(Utrecht *c*1570 – Prague 1613)
Tazza with Susanna and the Elders,
1612
Silver-gilt, diameter 20.6 cm
Acquired from Coll. D. G. van
Beuningen 1958; inv. MBZ196

2
Northern Netherlands
Tulip tile picture, *c*1640
Maiolica, 26.8 × 64 cm (total)
Acquired 1958; inv. A5030

3
Marinus van Gelder
Rummer with lid, 1659
Glass with diamond engraving,
height 38 cm
A. van Hoboken Bequest 1922; inv. 69

5

Michiel de Bruyn van
Berendrecht
Utrecht *c*1608 – London(?) before
1670)
Salt-cellar, 1650
Silver, height 20.2 cm
Gift 1978; inv. MBZ322

5
Hoppesteyn studio, Delft,
Netherlands; Silver: G. Prick,
Maastricht
Jug with silver lid, *c*1675
Earthenware, silver, height 27 cm
Gift 1980; inv. A5167

1

2

3

1

Meissen, Germany
Tea service, c1750
Porcelain
Philips-van der Willigen Bequest
1942; inv. A3207

2

Chine de Commande, 18th century
Dish with the arms of Frederick the
Great of Prussia
Porcelain, diameter 38.7 cm
Acquired 1958; inv. A3532

3

**Mount: Johann Simon Rothaer,
Hamburg**
Lady Harvey's Glass, c1708
Glass, silver-gilt, height 63 cm
Dr E. van Rijckevorsel Bequest 1928;
inv. 99
This imposing rummer is named
after the Englishwoman from whose
collection it came. The city of Hamburg, seen across the water, is illuminated on one side by a radiant sun
and on the other by a crescent moon
in a starry sky. The stem is embellished with wheel-engraved mer-
maids and dancing figures, prunts of
glass serving as faces. The exuberant
decoration climaxes in the elab-
orately worked silver-gilt foot and
lid, both by the Hamburg goldsmith
Johann Simon Rothaer, whose only
extant work this is. The lid is surmounted by a youthful Bacchus
seated on a cask garlanded with vine
tendrils. In one hand he is holding
grapes, with the other he trium-
phantly raises a glass aloft. The decoration of this enormous glass is thus
in keeping with its function: a
triumph of Bacchus and a triumph of
wine.

4

**Netherlands; action: Lourens
Eichelar, Amsterdam**
Standing clock, c1750
Walnut root wood, height 215 cm
Gift of Mrs M. C. van Nispen tot
Pannerden-Blankenheym 1912;
inv. Div.M.25

4

83

1

2

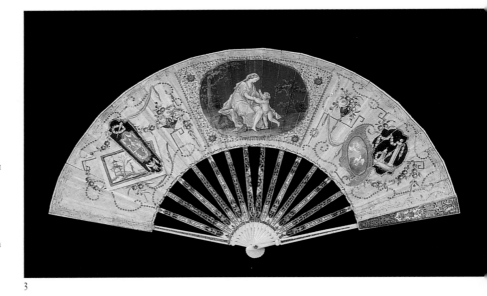

1

**Diederik Lodewijk Bennewitz,
Amsterdam**
Two chestnut vases, 1819
Silver, height 30 cm
Acquired 1968; inv. MBZ241 and 242

2

Netherlands, end 18th century
Goblet with stipple engraving of
Liberty
Glass, height 25 cm
Gift of A. van Hoboken, 1922; inv. 151

3

End 18th century
Fan
Ivory, painted silk, length 28.4 cm
Gift of Mr and Mrs de Monchy-van
der Hoeven, 1958; inv. D43

4

**G. W. van Dokkum
firm of J. M. van Kempen,
Voorschoten, Netherlands**
Candelabrum, 1864
Silver, height 66 cm
Acquired 1989; inv. MBZ394

3

5
Victor Barbizet (?), France
Oval dish, c1860
Earthenware, diameter 44 cm
Acquired 1943; inv. A4100

6
Austria (?), 2nd half 19th century
Jewellery casket
Rock crystal, silver-gilt, enamel, height 25.5 cm
Gift of Dr. E. van Rijckevorsel, 1910; inv. 936

In the course of the nineteenth century the stylistic unity of earlier movements was superseded by a wide diversity of forms and decorative motifs. Designs for decorative and useful objects were inspired by a variety of styles from the past; Gothic, Renaissance and Rococo were especially popular. Historicism was severely criticized for corrupting these stylistic elements. From the second half of the nineteenth century on, reforming tendencies such as the English Arts and Crafts Movement endeavoured to reinstate the craftsman and improve

4

5

the quality of decorative art. Neo-styles remained taboo until well into the twentieth century. For a long time the museums, too, banished much of this nineteenth-century work from their galleries, decrying its lack of originality and its over-elaborate workmanship. The brightly coloured relief dish in the manner of sixteenth-century Palissy earthenware and the Renaissance-style crystal jewellery casket illustrated here only came to the museum when they did because they were not recognized as nineteenth-century work. Only in the past few decades has there been a revived interest in objects which reflect the taste and aspirations of the emerging bourgeoisie: the ornate silver candelabrum, one of a pair, was deliberately acquired with this aspect in mind.

6

1
A. F. Gips (1861–1943)
Koninklijke Utrechtse Fabriek voor Zilverwerken C. J. Begeer, Utrecht
Coffee and tea service, 1900
Silver
Gift 1985; inv. MBZ370

2
William Morris
(Walthamstow 1834 – Kelmscott 1896)
Curtain fabric, *Bird*, 1878 (detail)
Double-weave wool, 70 × 150 cm
Acquired 1985; inv. V2.8.-1470

3
Jan Eisenloeffel
(Amsterdam 1876 – Amsterdam 1957)
Pendant lamp, 1923
Tombak, enamel, height 180 cm
Gift of A. W. Goudriaan 1982;
inv. V2.2-1399
This huge pendant lamp, made of tombak (a copper and zinc alloy), was commissioned by the Rotterdam shipowner A. J. M. Goudriaan. Inspired by the ideas of Freud and Darwin, Eisenloeffel took man's basic urges as the theme of the representation on the enamel friezes: self-preservation and the survival of the species. These two urges are linked with the four seasons and depicted in agricultural and hunting scenes and representations of amatory and spiritual life. The heavy, pagoda-shaped lamp is hard to reconcile with the plain, functional design of Eisenloeffel's precious metal services from the turn of the century. Originally a pioneer of modern design in the Netherlands, by about 1909 Eisenloeffel had turned into a craftsman who clung to traditional methods. He worked for a select group of wealthy customers, of whom Goudriaan was the most important. This lamp is surely his most ambitious project, sparing neither cost nor effort. Indeed, it turned out to be so expensive that it caused a lengthy rift in the relationship between client and artist.

1

2

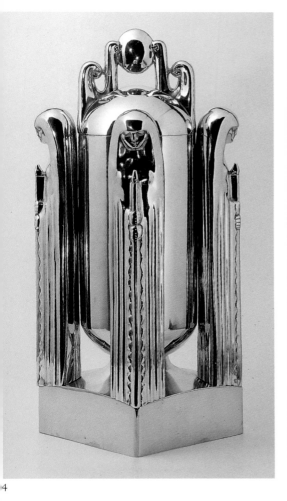

4

3

5

4
Hendrik Albertus van den Eijnde
(Haarlem 1869 – Haarlem 1939);
Firma J. M. van Kempen,
Voorschoten
Urn, 1918
Silver, height 60 cm
Acquired 1982; inv. MBZ348

5
J. J. Kok; decoration: R. Sterken
Haagse Koninklijke Porselein- en
Aardewerkfabriek Rozenburg,
The Hague
Vase, 1903
Eggshell porcelain, height 30 cm
Acquired 1954; inv. A3092

1
Jacob Jongert
(Wormer 1883 – Wormer 1942);
De Erven de Wed. J. Van Nelle,
Rotterdam
Storage tin, 1930
Tin, 37 × 41.5 × 28 cm
Acquired 1986; inv. V4.5-1007

2
L. C. Kalff
NV Philips
Gloeilampenfabrieken,
Eindhoven, Netherlands

Radio set *2502*, 1927
Metal, rexine, phenolformaldehyde,
diameter 44 cm
Acquired 1983; inv. V2.5-912

1

2

Industrial design in the Boymans Museum

Since the early 1980s the museum
has pursued an active collecting
policy in the field of industrial
design. As well as assembling a basic
collection of objects considered to be
representative for the history of
international design, the museum
focuses on two specific areas: the
working environment and leisure
activities. In the first of these –
which, besides office furniture, lamps
and desk accessories also presents
apparatus – Olivetti occupies a
prominent place. Mario Bellini
designed *Divisumma*, the calculator
illustrated here, for the Italian company in 1973. The machine is tilted
for convenient reading and operation; the keys are made of soft
rubber; user-friendliness is a para-
mount consideration. The collection
of leisure items includes sports
accessories, bicycles, radios and tele-
vision sets. Here, too, the focus is on
products expressing an explicit
design ideology or an innovative
vision. A good example is
Brompton's folding bicycle, which
went into production in 1986. The
smallest of its kind, it is not only distinguished by its compact design but
handles extremely well on the road.

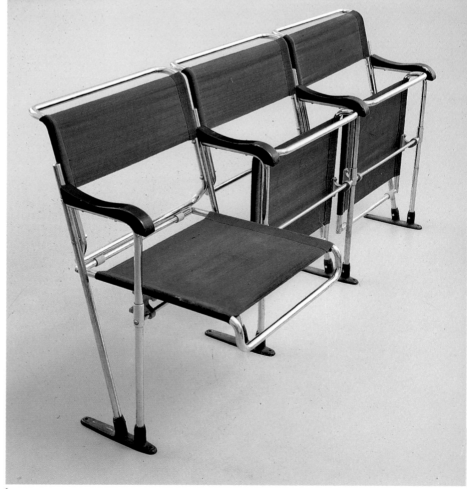

3

3
Marcel Breuer
(Pecs 1902 – New York 1981);
Gebr. Thonet, Frankenberg
Three linked folding chairs, 1926
Chromium-plated tubular steel, iron
thread, wood, height 85.6 cm
On loan from a private collection;
inv. V2.1-1623

4
Marianne Brandt
(Chemnitz 1893 – Kirchberg 1983);
Ruppelwerk Metallwarenfabrik
GmbH, Gotha, Germany
Inkwell, 1931
Sheet steel, glass, height 4.5 cm
Acquired 1990; inv. V6.2-1469

5
Julian Vereker, Andrew Richie
Brompton Bicycle Ltd, Great
Britain
Brompton folding bicycle, 1978
(design), 1986 (production)
Carbon, steel, height 56.5 cm
Acquired 1991; inv. V4.2-1593

4

6

7

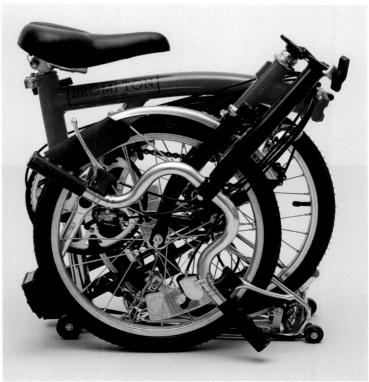

5

6
Mario Bellini
(born Milan 1935);
Ing. C. Olivetti & Co SpA, Italy
Divisumma 28 calculator, 1973
Rubber, metal, length 17 cm
Acquired 1984; inv. v6.3-267

7
James Dyson (born 1947)
Apex Inc, Japan
Cyclon vacuum cleaner, 1979 (design),
1985 (production)
Plastic, height 100 cm
Acquired 1987; Inv. V3.4-812

1
Andries Dirk Copier
(Leerdam 1901 – Wassenaar 1991);
Leerdam Unica
Bottle, 1958
Glass, height 36.6 cm
Acquired 1958; inv. 704

Andries Dirk Copier may rightfully be regarded as the 'grand old man' of Dutch glassware. In the more than 55 years that he worked at the Leerdam glasshouse he produced hundreds of designs for glassware series. From the 1920s to the 1950s virtually no Dutch household was without some item of his work. Millions of his *Gilde* glasses, designed shortly before 1930 in association with the Dutch Association of Wine-Merchants and still in production, are distributed all over the world. Besides these activities, Copier began to make one-offs in 1923, one

1

2

2
Hans Coper
(Chemnitz 1920 – Frome, Somerset
1981)
Spade form, 1966
Stoneware, height 44.5 cm
Acquired 1967; inv. A4477

3
Alison Britton
(born London 1948)
Pot, 1988
Earthenware, height 29 cm
Acquired 1991; inv. A6593

3

of the first Dutch glass designers to do so. These unique pieces were the result of close collaboration between designer and glass-blower; the museum owns fifty of them. This blue bottle of 1958 was one of Copier's own favourites and won an award at an exhibition in America.

The distinctive dent was caused by applying heat locally to the spherical form, after which the glass-blower sucked instead of blowing. Copier decided on a green spot in the otherwise blue glass to mark this operation.

4

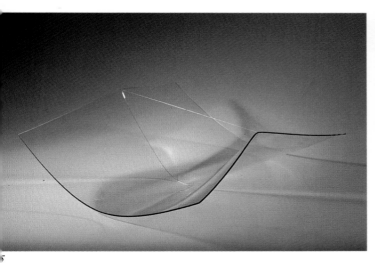

5

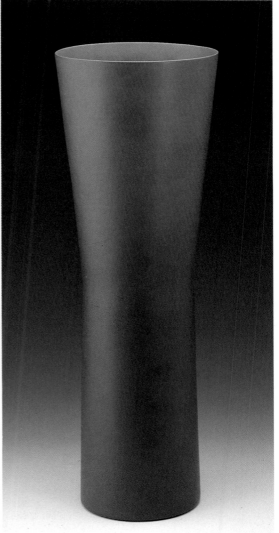

6

4
Lino Tagliapietra
(born Murano 1934)
Bowl, 1987
Glass, height 16 cm, diameter 32 cm
Acquired 1988; inv. 1912

5
Bert Frijns
(born Kerkrade, 1953)
Object, 1986
Glass, wire, 16.4 × 46.2 × 48.3 cm
Acquired 1986; inv. 1891

6
Geert Lap
(born Venlo 1951)
Vase, 1988
Terra Sigillata, height 49.2 cm
Acquired 1988; inv. A6091

I

2
Cologne
Jar, c1550
Stoneware, height 20.2 cm
van Beuningen-de Vriese collection,
1983
inv. F3968

3
North Holland
Fire cover, 1686
Red earthenware, yellow slip
decoration, height 21.7 cm
van Beuningen-de Vriese collection,
1983
inv. F7724
From medieval times fire covers
with a small opening at the top to
admit air were used to prevent fires
going out overnight. The example
illustrated here is dated 1686 and
bears the text *Vreest. Godt. Hout. Sin.
Geboode. En. Dient. Geen. Aardse.
Gooden. Die. Noch. Toe. Sach*, roughly
translating as 'fear God, keep his
commandments and serve no other
gods'. The stylized pomegranates at
the top are fertility symbols. The

cover was probably a wedding present. The text and decoration were
applied to the unfired earthenware
with the aid of a cow's horn, which
served as a dispenser for the runny
paste of white pipe-clay. Slip dec-
orations, common since the Middle
Ages, were particularly suitable for
red earthenware. Stoneware, with its
finer and firmer structure, was often
decorated in relief, applied with a
mould, a technique used for the
motif of oak branches and acorns on
the sixteenth-century jar illustrated
here, which comes from Cologne
where such clay was common.
Stoneware is less resistant to heat
than earthenware, which is why
most objects from Cologne are
drinking and pouring vessels.

3

4
Netherlands, 18th century
Ocarinas
Earthenware, height 10.3 cm, 15.4 cm
and 7.7 cm
Van Beuningen-de Vriese collection;
inv. F4334, F681, F3318

Department of Modern Art

Willem van Rede (1880-1953)

The Rotterdam collector Willem van Rede played a special role in the museum's history. The museum is less indebted to him for his collections than for the Fund that bears his name and whose capital swells the museum's holdings.

Willem van Rede regarded himself as a full-blooded collector: 'What is collecting? In a word: passion.' The only limits he acknowledged were the capacity of his purse and his house. He was both a systematic and catholic collector in such widely divergent fields as ethnography, paleontology, prehistory, fine and decorative art, numismatics, naturalia, lepidoptera, entomology, philately and books.

After his father's death in 1924, van Rede had enough money to retire from the family grain business in Rotterdam and devote himself exclusively to his two great loves: collecting and travel. His visits to museums and exhibitions in numerous cities, documented by chronologically ordered picture postcards, served to develop his taste and increase his knowledge. His 'Itineraria', diaries of his trips, endorse his conviction that a collector should rely on his own expert judgement. After his wanderlust had taken him to such remote places as Morocco, Palestine, The Lebanon, Syria and Turkey between 1925 and 1928, van Rede moved into the family residence on Schiekade, Rotterdam, with his much younger French wife, Adrienne Langlais. Henceforth, he was only to leave Rotterdam for brief excursions to Paris and lengthier sojourns in the couple's second home in the south of France.

Van Rede bought items for his collections on his travels and from dealers in Rotterdam and The Hague. Every year he went to Paris for the annual *Salon*. Quantity often seems to have outweighed quality: van Rede had a predilection for conventional nineteenth-century paintings which were regrettably mediocre. He was an impulse buyer, often purchasing works of art by the dozen and never without haggling; visiting Paris in 1925 and 1926, he bought 80 canvases by various minor painters. Towards the end of the decade he acquired a few more valuable seventeenth-century paintings, hoping to vie with Rotterdam's most distinguished collectors, van Beuningen and van der Vorm.

Convinced of the importance of his collections, the childless van Rede did his utmost to ensure that they would not be dispersed after his death. He died in 1953, leaving his collections to the Rotterdam museums, the Municipal Archive, the Public Library and Blijdorp Zoo. He seemed to have set greater store by his paintings and drawings, coins and medals, which he bequeathed to the nation. The nation has since passed on some of these drawings to the Boymans Museum, to which van Rede had left a number of ceramic pieces outright. The paintings, of disappointing quality, remained in the care of the nation: many a winter landscape and nocturnal scene from the van Rede collection adorns the walls of Dutch embassies!

According to the terms of van Rede's will, his entire capital was to be used by the Boymans Museum for the purchase of work by contemporary Rotterdam and foreign artists. Since 1956 this Fund has enabled the museum to purchase 25 important pieces which have greatly enhanced its holdings. The works represent a wide range of movements. At first the accent was on expressionist paintings such as Oskar Kokoschka's *Double Portrait*, Alexey Jawlensky's *Study of a Nude* and Raoul Dufy's *Carriage in the Bois de Boulogne*. In the late 1970s and early 1980s the focus shifted to minimal art: acquisitions include significant sculptures such as Richard Serra's *Waxing Arcs*, Carl Andre's *Forty-Ninth Steel Cardinal* and Donald Judd's *Galvanized Iron 17th January*. More recent additions to the museum's holdings of surrealism and contemporary German painting are works by Marcel Duchamp and Gerhard Richter. Fate has thus taken an ironical twist in linking van Rede's name irrevocably with modern art, with which he himself had little affinity.

Edward James (1907-1984)

Edward James left his mark on the museum with more than just its collection of works by Dali and Magritte, all but two of which were purchased from him. René Magritte's two portraits of the rich, eccentric poet–collector provide an unforgettable picture of the James we know from contemporary descriptions: an exceedingly elegant young man, willowy and well-dressed, whose shirts came from Italy and ties from Paris. But Magritte also shows him as the incarnation of surrealist ideas. The famous *Reproduction Forbidden* shows James in front of a looking-glass, which reflects, surrealistically, the *back* of his head, a repetition which prevents us from seeing his face. *La Maison de Verre* is an equally unconventional portrait: again we see the back of James' head, in which his face looms up.

Although Edward James owned dozens of Dalis and Magrittes, as well as paintings by Picasso, De Chirico and Tchelitchew, he was not driven by the true collector's passion; he saw himself first and foremost as a patron, the role he played for Dali and Magritte in particular during the 1930s. Rumoured to be an illegitimate son of King Edward VII, he grew up in an eleventh-century castle on the West Dean estate near Chichester, in the south of England. At the age of 21 the young man inherited fortunes from his father and his uncle. Having broken off his studies at Oxford and made an unsuccessful debut in diplomatic circles, he henceforth

The first floor of van Rede's house on Schiekade, Rotterdam

René Magritte, *The House of Glass*, 1939, gouache

marriage brought James into contact with the Parisian dance and music avant garde. With his wife's career in mind, he commissioned music from Darius Milhaud and Kurt Weill and choreographies from Georges Balanchine, whose company 'Les Ballets 1933' he rescued from dire financial straits. It was during this period that James entered surrealist circles. From 1933 he sponsored the famous surrealist review *Minotaure*, in which he published a few essays and poems with illustrations by Salvador Dali. The two men shared a love of the bizarre and extravagant, and embarked on an intense friendship. Together they travelled to Italy and in 1939 visited Sigmund Freud in London.

In 1938 James engaged Dali to wreak a surrealist metamorphosis on Monkton, the country cottage built in 1907 by Edwin Lutyens on the West Dean estate in which James had spent many a childhood hour in the company of his sisters and governess. In his role of patron James went so far as to have a contract drawn up in 1936 which pledged him to make Dali a generous allowance for the painter's output from 1936 to 1938, an agreement that was to have catastrophic consequences for their friendship.

James' relationship with René Magritte was on a more even keel; he was the Belgian surrealist's most important collector and patron in the 1930s. During his stay at James' London home in Wimpole Street, Magritte not only painted the celebrated *Reproduction Forbidden* but at James' request made him a second version of *Le Modèle Rouge*.

In 1939 James broke with most of his contacts and departed for America, where he frequented Hollywood's literary and homosexual demi-monde. Eventually he exchanged this scene for a secluded life in Xilitla in Mexico, where he built a conglomeration of fantastic architectural structures in the middle of the jungle.

James' surrealist paintings remained hidden away at West Dean. At the end of the 1960s the then senior curator of the Boymans-van Beuningen Museum, Renilde Hammacher-van den Brande, procured a number of works by Dali on loan for a retrospective. At the opening in November 1970 the painter, deeply moved, saw these works for the first time in many years. Two years later, to mark the opening of the new wing, James loaned the museum 25 works by Magritte and Dali; various funds enabled the purchase in 1977 and 1979 of twelve of the paintings, drawings and gouaches from the two painters' most productive period.

During this period James sold most of his other works of art, which are now scattered over different collections. On his death the surrealist Monkton cottage was dismantled and auctioned to finance a project dear to James' heart, a school for traditional crafts which he had founded at West Dean.

devoted himself exclusively to the pleasures of a free, luxurious life. His Bohemian lifestyle hampered his serious development as a poet, and his volumes of verse did not always meet with critical acclaim. In 1931 he founded the James Press, which brought out not only most of his own work – including his only novel, *The Gardener Who Saw God* 1937) – but also *Mount Zion*, the first volume of poems by his friend John Betjeman, whom James greatly admired.

In 1928 James became enamoured of the Viennese ballet dancer Tilly Losch, whom he met in London when she was performing in a Noël Coward revue. Their brief, unhappy

1

2

96

3
Edgar Degas
(Paris 1834 – Paris 1917)
Little dancer, fourteen years old, 1880/81
Bronze, muslin and satin, height
98 cm
Purchased 1939; inv. St9/Bek 1239

4
George Hendrik Breitner
(Rotterdam 1857 – Amsterdam 1923)
The Earring, 1893
Oil on canvas, 84.5 × 57.5 cm
Gift of W. H. de Monchy and the
Erasmus Foundation 1952; inv. St95

4

Alfred Sisley
Paris 1839 – Moret-sur-Loing
1899)
The Watermill Provencher at Moret,
883
Oil on canvas, 54 × 93 cm
Mrs A. E. van Beuningen-Charlouis
Bequest 1981; inv. 3023
Impressionism, represented by
paintings of Monet, Pissarro and
Sisley, is one of the focal points of
the museum's collection. Sisley
painted this superb landscape in 1883
in Moret-sur-Loing, a small town

south-east of Paris at the confluence
of the Loing and the Seine. To capture the fleeting effects of light in
the sky and on the water, Sisley, like
many other Impressionists, painted
his canvases on the spot. The
reflections in the water are rendered
in tiny strokes of paint. The
washerwomen on the riverbank are
little more than coloured accents.
The mill and footbridge are tranquil
elements amidst all this sparkling
colour. Sisley painted the wooden
bridge in perspective, creating an
illusion of depth which other
Impressionists sought to suppress.

2
Claude Monet
(Paris 1840 – Giverny 1926)
Fisherman's cabin at Varengeville, 1882
Oil on canvas, 60 × 78 cm
Acquired with the van der Schilden
Bequest 1928; inv. 1544

97

1

2

3

4

1
Paul Signac
(Paris 1863 – Paris 1935)
The Port of Rotterdam, 1907
Oil on canvas, 87 × 114 cm
Gift of Dr D. Hannema 1952;
inv. St96
Fascinated by the *'ballet tumultueux de la Meuse'*, Signac painted this harbour view a year after his visit to Rotterdam in 1906. The bustling activity of the harbour is painted from an unusually high viewpoint in broad, identical dabs of colour. The bridge in the background is the Willemsbrug. For the sake of the composition, the area called Noordereiland (North Island) and the church on Stieltjesplein is pictured on the left instead of the right. Unlike the Impressionists, Signac painted all his divisionist canvases in the studio, working up drawings and watercolours done out of doors beforehand. The museum owns one of these watercolours: it is splashed with paint, showing that the artist kept it within reach while he was painting in the studio.

2
Aristide Maillol
(Banyuls-sur-Mer 1861 – Marly-le-Roy 1944)
La Méditerranée, 1902–05
Bronze, 110 × 77.5 × 113 cm
Presented by the combined industries of Rotterdam and the Rotterdam Friends of the Museum 1961; inv. Bek 1401

3
Edouard Vuillard
(Cuisseaux 1868 – La Baule 1940)
Woman in pink, knitting, c1900–05
Body colour on cardboard,
26 × 16.5 cm
The Vitale Bloch Bequest 1976;
inv. 2897

4
Vincent van Gogh
(Zundert 1853 – Auvers-sur-Oise 1890)
Armand Roulin, 1888
Oil on canvas, 65 × 54 cm
Coll. D. G. van Beuningen 1958;
inv. 2608
At the end of February 1888 van Gogh left Paris for Arles, where he made friends with the postman Joseph Roulin and his family. Van Gogh was fascinated by portraiture at this time, wanting to do for portraits 'what Claude Monet had done for the landscape'. The Roulins proved to be rewarding models. Van Gogh's first portrait of the postman was followed in November and December 1888 by a whole series, one of which was the mother in *La Berceuse*. As well as this picture of the Roulins' 17-year-old son Armand, van Gogh painted a full-face portrait now in the Folkwang-museum, Essen. The composition and colouring of this portrait are simple and direct. Instead of the decorative elements often used by van Gogh in the backgrounds of his other portraits, he opted for an even, bright green area against which the young man stands out in firm outlines.

99

1

2
**Oskar Kokoschka
(Pöchlarn 1886 – Montreux 1980)**
Double portrait, 1919
Oil on canvas, 100.5 × 143 cm
W. van Rede Fund 1956; inv. 2419,
2420
In this double portrait Kokoschka
endeavoured to express the friendship of two very different personali-
ties. The man on the left is the
lawyer Hans Mardersteig (1892-1977),
who later founded the famous printing house Officina Bodoni in Verona;
on the right is the art historian Carl
George Heise (1890-1979), champion
of the expressionists and later
museum director in Lübeck and
Hamburg. As in a diptych, each is
depicted in his own space. Pose and
colouring are important factors in
the portrayal of the two characters.
The extrovert Heise is rendered in
green, pink and red, while the intro-
vert Mardersteig is dominated by
deep blue. Kokoschka used vivid
yellow and orange in the latter's face
to express 'the inner fire of this
withdrawn man'.

3
**Alexej Jawlensky
(Torsjok 1864 – Wiesbaden 1941)**
*Study of a nude, c*1910
Oil on cardboard, 99 × 69.5 cm
W. van Rede Fund 1960; inv. 2624

4
**Kees van Dongen
(Delfshaven 1877 – Monte Carlo
1968)**
Finger on the cheek, 1910
Oil on canvas, 65 × 54 cm
Gift of Mrs L. de Graaff-Bachiene
1949/50; inv. St78

1
**Edvard Munch
(Engehaug near Løyten, 1863 –
Ekely, near Oslo, 1944)**
Two girls and an apple tree in bloom,
1905
Oil on canvas, 130 × 110 cm
Purchased 1957; inv. 2426

2

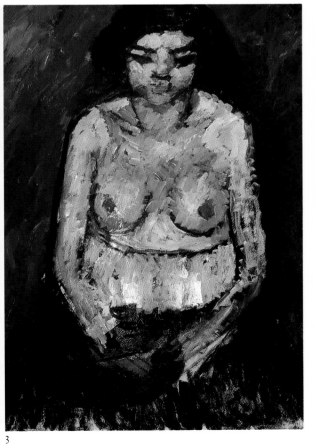

3

4

1

1
**Wassily Kandinsky
(Moscow 1866 – Neuilly-sur-Seine
1944)**
Large study, 1914
Oil on canvas, 100.5 × 79 cm
Purchased 1964; inv. 2677

2
**Wassily Kandinsky
(Moscow 1866 – Neuilly-sur-Seine
1944)**
Lyrisches, 1911
Oil on canvas, 94 × 130 cm
M. Tak van Poortvliet Bequest,
Domburg 1936; inv. 1430
The museum owns thirteen works
by Wassily Kandinsky, ranging from
an early, fairy-tale representation of
1904 to a painting of 1935 which
employs the organic, abstract
vocabulary so typical of the period.

A highlight in this group of paintings is *Lyrisches* of 1911. The central
theme is a horseman, one of Kandinsky's favourite motifs during this
period. With a few expressive lines
and insubstantial clouds of colour
Kandinsky evokes the sensation of
speed in infinite space in a work
which hovers on the border of
abstraction and figuration.
The painting was purchased before
1921 by Marie Tak van Poortvliet, a
collector with progressive opinions
and an international outlook.

2

Visitors to Loverendale, her country estate near Domburg in the province of Zeeland, included not only Piet Mondrian and Jacoba van Heemskerk but also the German champion of modern art, Herwardt Walden. Thanks to her contacts with Walden, who organized exhibitions in Berlin and published the review *Der Sturm*, Marie Tak van Poortvliet acquired several modern masterpieces. Along with Kandinsky's *Lyrisches*, she left Franz Marc's *Lamb* and Lyonel Feininger's *Ober-Weimar* to the museum in 1936.

3
Lyonel Feininger
(New York 1871 – New York 1956)
Ober–Weimar, 1921
Oil on canvas, 90 × 100 cm
M. Tak van Poortvliet Bequest,
Domburg 1936; inv. 1217

3

1

Surrealism

With the purchase in 1965 of Max Ernst's *The Couple* (1923) and René Magritte's *On the Threshold of Freedom* (1929), the museum embarked on a collection of surrealist art that is unique in the Netherlands. In the 1970s a homogeneous ensemble of fifteen works was acquired from the collection of poet and collector Edward James, the most important patron of Salvador Dali and René Magritte in the 1930s. Dali and Magritte represent only one facet of a movement whose politics, too, were revolutionary and in which writers, poets and artists, under the leadership of André Breton, enthusiastically championed the irrational and the imaginative. Images dredged up from the subconscious were accurately registered in an almost photographic manner. Fascinated by the writings of Freud, Dali developed the process which he referred to as 'active, paranoiac critical' as a means of addressing the irrational in a deliberate fashion. In Magritte's work surprising combinations of images, often with enigmatic titles, completely undermine a commonplace object's ostensible meaning or the apparent familiarity of a situa-

2

tion. The conceptual side of surrealism is illustrated by the more recent
acquisition of several multiples by
Marcel Duchamp, including *La
Boîte-en-valise*. The valise is an
eloquent example of this inspiring
artist's outlook, which was as acute
as it was radical, the views of a man
who did not mean his art to delight
the eye but to jog the mind.

1
René Magritte
(**Lessen 1898 – Brussels 1967**)
Le Modèle Rouge II, 1937
Oil on canvas, 183 × 136 cm
Purchased from the Edward James
Foundation with the support of the
Rembrandt Association, the Prince
Bernhard Fund, the Erasmus Foun-
dation, the Stichting Bevordering
van Volkskracht Rotterdam and the

Boymans-van Beuningen Museum
Foundation 1979; inv. 2992

2
René Magritte
(**Lessen 1898 – Brussels 1967**)
Reproduction Forbidden, 1937
Oil on canvas, 81 × 65 cm
Purchased from Edward James 1977;
inv. 2939

1

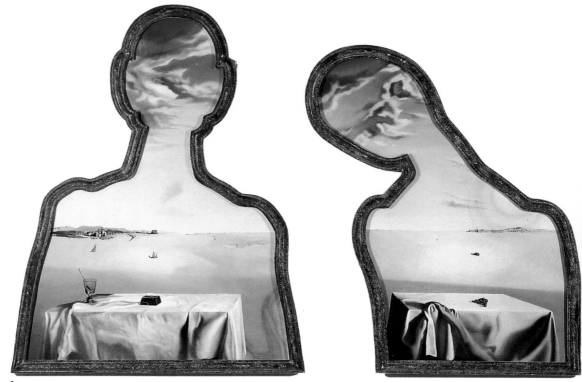

2

3
Marcel Duchamp
(Blainville 1887 – Neuilly-sur-
Seine 1968)
La boîte-en-valise, 1952
Leather case with replicas and

black/white and colour
reproductions, 41 × 37.8 × 10.5 cm
Purchased with support from the
W. van Rede Fund 1990;
inv. MB1990/1

4
Man Ray
(Philadelphia 1890 – Paris 1976)
The enigma of Isidore Ducasse, 1920/71
Sewing machine wrapped in a
blanket, 45 × 58 × 23 cm
Purchased 1972; inv. Bek 1491

1
Salvador Dali
(Figueras 1904 – Barcelona 1989)
Impressions d'Afrique, 1938
Oil on canvas, 91.5 × 117.5 cm
Purchased from the Edward James
Foundation with the support of the

Rembrandt Association, the Prince
Bernhard Fund, the Erasmus
Foundation, Stichting Bevordering
van Volkskracht Rotterdam and the
Boymans-van Beuningen Museum
Foundation 1979; inv. 2991
Impressions d'Afrique is the title of a
book, published in 1910, by Ray-
mond Roussel, whom the surrealists
greatly admired. Dali's painting has
nothing to do with the book; the
only connection is that neither tells
a coherent story and that Dali's
technique is as conventional and
academic as Roussel's language. In
the left foreground Dali – in one of
his few self-portraits – sits at his
easel, his hand outstretched in a
dramatic gesture; he is gazing out of
the picture with a tense expression
on his face. In the background we
see the double images produced by
the 'paranoiac critical process',
images which can be read in more
than one way. Here they form
arcades in the landscape and the
eye-sockets of Gala, Dali's wife and
muse. Dali painted *Impressions d'Afri-*
que in Rome in 1938, following a brief

sojourn in Sicily which, as he wrote
in his autobiography, reminded him
both of his native Catalonia and of
Africa. Dali, however, had never
been in Africa; it was the arid Cata-
lan coast around Port Lligat,
Cadaques and Cape Creus which
supplied the landscape decor for his
paintings.

2
Salvador Dali
(Figueras 1904 – Barcelona 1989)
Couple with their heads full of clouds,
1936
Oil on panel, 92.5 × 69.5 cm (man),
82.5 × 62.5 cm (woman)
Purchased from the Edward James
Foundation with the support of the
Rembrandt Association, the Prince
Bernhard Fund, the Erasmus
Foundation, Stichting Bevordering
van Volkskracht Rotterdam and the
Boymans-van Beuningen Museum
Foundation 1979; inv. 2988

Pyke Koch
(**Beek** 1901 – **Utrecht** 1991)
The shooting gallery, 1931
Oil on canvas, 170 × 130 cm
Gift of Mrs D. Hintzen-s' Jacob,
C. H. van der Leeuw, M. A. G. van
der Leeuw, J. Mees and H. Nijgh,
Rotterdam 1931; inv. 1425

I

'In magic realism the representations are possible but not probable, whereas surrealism depicts situations which are impossible, do not or cannot exist.' This was how Koch summed up the movement under which his work is classified. His large paintings are characterized by a meticulous technique and a harsh light which relentlessly exposes every detail. *The shooting gallery* is fraught with Freudian eroticism; the larger-than-life, slightly repulsive woman is so overwhelmingly present that she seems to be offering herself as the target. The impression is reinforced by her unyielding yet provocative attitude and blatant physicality, and is further enhanced by the rifles on her right. In his poem *The Shooting Gallery*, Martinus Nijhoff, a close friend of the artist, compares the prostitute and mother motifs. Koch may have had this contrast in mind when he started on *Anna* (1932-35), an unfinished portrait of the opposite, affective female type: a gentle, wistful, old-maidish young woman.

2
Charley Toorop
(Katwijk aan Zee 1891 – Bergen
(N-H) 1957)
Three generations, 1941-50
Oil on canvas, 200 × 121 cm
Acquired with funds collected by the people of Rotterdam and with the support of the Erasmus Foundation and W. H. de Monchy 1951; inv. 2345
In this painting, which it took nine years to complete, Charley Toorop portrayed her family in her characteristic, expressively realistic style. Using sober, wintry colours she assembled her father, the painter Jan Toorop, her son Eddy Fernhout, also a painter, and herself into a closely knit composition. An imposing bronze head made by sculptor John Raedacker in 1932, also in the collection, stood model for her father. The artist's purpose was not to bring out the common characteristics of the three sitters but their individual traits, and each portrait was painted in a different manner. The work has a direct impact: the persons are depicted frontally, at close range, the artist's active attitude contrasting with the static poses of her father and son. Close-up and cropping are devices which Charley Toorop borrowed from modern German and Russian film, while the theme adheres to the Dutch portrait tradition.

2

CoBrA

Attesting to the great vitality which arose from the ashes of World War II, writers, poets and artists from Copenhagen, Brussels and Amsterdam collaborated on an international scale for the short period 8 November 1948 to November 1951. The museum holds a solid CoBrA nucleus, consisting of work by Appel, Constant, Rooskens, Asger Jorn and Lotti van der Gaag. The collective aspect dominated. Under the leadership of the Belgian writer Dotremont a lively activity developed: *CoBrA* magazine, books and booklets were published, exhilarating and sensational exhibitions such as one at the Stedelijk Museum in Amsterdam were mounted, and there were also inspiring projects in Denmark. CoBrA launched a new mentality, a new method, new ideas. Breaking with the aesthetic of the Paris school, CoBrA artists painted children and animals, monsters and masks, fanciful landscapes and cities,

in a fresh, original style. Their inspiration came from children's drawings, folk art and so-called primitive cultures, which are distinguished chiefly by their spontaneity. CoBrA painting is extremely expressive – colour and its application were more than just a means of representation: they acquired autonomy as a powerful handwriting, registering emotion and imagination.

1
Constant
(born Amsterdam 1920)
Mother and child, 1951
Oil on canvas, 115 × 146 cm
Purchased 1965; inv. 2702

2
Karel Appel
(born Amsterdam 1921)
Farmer with a donkey and pail, 1950
Oil on part of a stable door, chain and pail, 138 × 102 cm
Gift of Architect H. A. Maaskant, Rotterdam 1978; inv. 2969

3
Pablo Picasso
(Malaga 1881 – Antibes 1973)
The couple, 1970
Oil on canvas, 114 × 87 cm
W. van Rede Fund 1982; inv. 3042

3

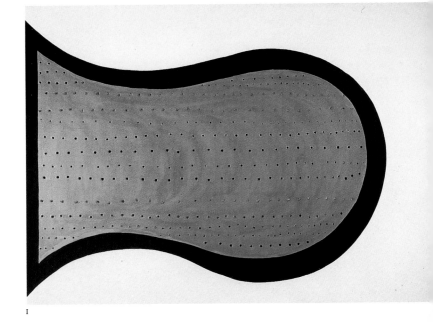

1

1
Lucio Fontana
(Rosario 1899 – Milan 1968)
Concetto Spaziale, 1954
Oil on canvas, 166 × 126 cm
Purchased 1968; inv. 2742

2
Bridget Riley
(born London 1931)
Breathe, 1966
Emulsion on canvas, 297 × 208 cm
Purchased 1971; inv. 2779

3
Mark Rothko
**(Dwinsk, Russia, 1903 – New York
1970)**
Grey, orange on maroon 60/8, 1960
Oil on canvas, 228 × 258.5 cm
Purchased 1970; inv. 2764
'I am not interested in relationships
of colour or form or anything else ...
I am interested only in expressing
the basic human emotions – tragedy,
ecstasy, doom and so on ...' Around
1950 Rothko found the basic form for
expressing mystical experience in
his work: the image is reduced to
virtually nothing; seemingly imma-
terial, unbordered colour-fields
detach themselves from the background. The symmetrical structure
makes his canvases into glowing
icons. Rothko preserved the strong
emotional intensity of this image for
twenty years, during which his work
evolved towards increasing simplic-
ity and reduction of colour.

2

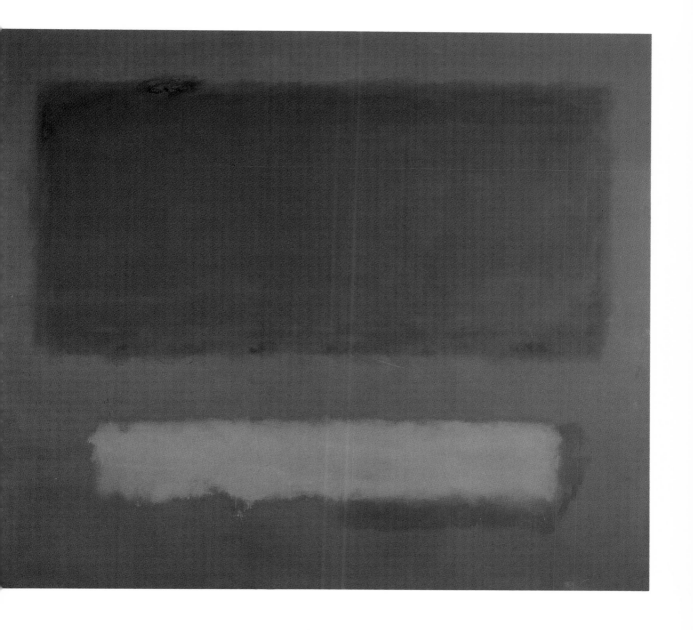

1

1

Claes Oldenburg
(born Stockholm 1929)
Screw Arch, 1982
Painted aluminium 386 × 655 cm,
head diameter 240 cm
Purchased 1982; inv. Bek1589
Between 1979 and 1983, at the
museum's request, the American
Pop artist Claes Oldenburg made
five works on the theme of the
screw. Inspired by construction
plans for the Willemsbrug, a bridge
across the river Maas in the centre
of Rotterdam, Oldenburg produced
a series of three etchings and a
bronze model. In these 'proposals for
a colossal monument', two huge
curved screws span the New Maas
like a bridge. The group of works
climaxed in a large sculpture in the
museum garden. Despite its plastic
and almost abstract qualities, the
screw remains a screw, surprising
the beholder that such an in-
significant object can attain such
proportions.

Andy Warhol
(Pittsburgh 1928 – New York 1987)
The Kiss (Bela Lugosi), 1963
serigraph on linen, 210 × 540 cm
Purchased 1979; inv. 2984

3

George Segal
(born New York 1924)
Couple at the stairs, 1964
Plaster, wood and metal,
305 × 264 × 244 cm
Purchased 1970; inv. Bek1453

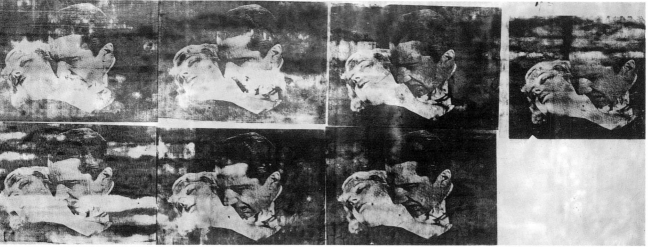

1

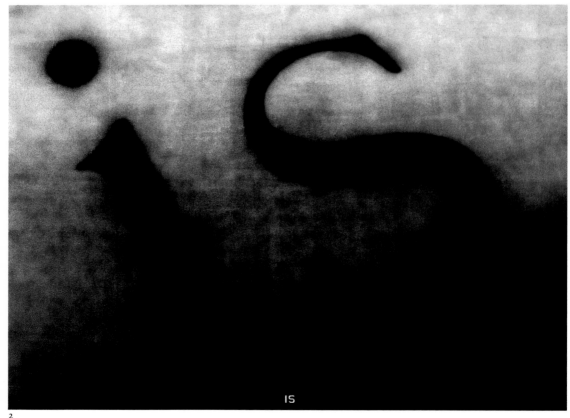

2

Bruce Nauman
(born Fort Wayne, Indiana 1941)
Studio piece, 1979
Plaster, wood, 90 × 420 × 300 cm
Purchased 1980; inv. Bek1570

Edward Ruscha
(born Omaha, Nebraska 1937)
Is, 1991
Acrylic on canvas, 173 × 200 cm
Purchased 1991; inv. 3257

3

3
Donald Judd
(born Excelsior Springs, Missouri 1928)
Untitled, 1984
Pigment, burnt into aluminium, 150 × 165 × 900 cm
Purchased with support from the Rembrandt Association 1987; inv. Bek1632

At the end of the 1960s a number of minimal artists such as Judd, Andre, Morris, Flavin and Grosvenor made a clean break with the principles of traditional sculpture. Abandoning the sculptor's craftsmanship, they had their works produced in factories from industrial materials. Eschewing emotional expression, they addressed elementary sculptural principles such as size, organization, structure, site and gravity. In particular, they stressed the sculpture's relationship with its surroundings by placing it directly on the ground, without a plinth. A number of these principles can still be observed in Donald Judd's recent untitled piece. The sculpture consists of singular, identical elements of geometrical shape. Unlike his earlier work, this sculpture has extreme proportions. Nine metres long, its height is attuned to human size and it enters into a compelling relationship with the surrounding space. Another difference is the abundant use of colour. These bright hues, obtained by burning the pigments into the aluminium, are organized in an apparently arbitrary fashion, thus averting the threat of massive monumentality.

Frank Stella
(born Malden, Massachusetts 1936)
Marsanxett Harbour (A1), 1983
Honeycomb aluminium, magnesium
and steel, painted and etched,
288 × 297 × 89 cm
Purchased with support from the
Rembrandt Association 1983;
inv. Bek1599

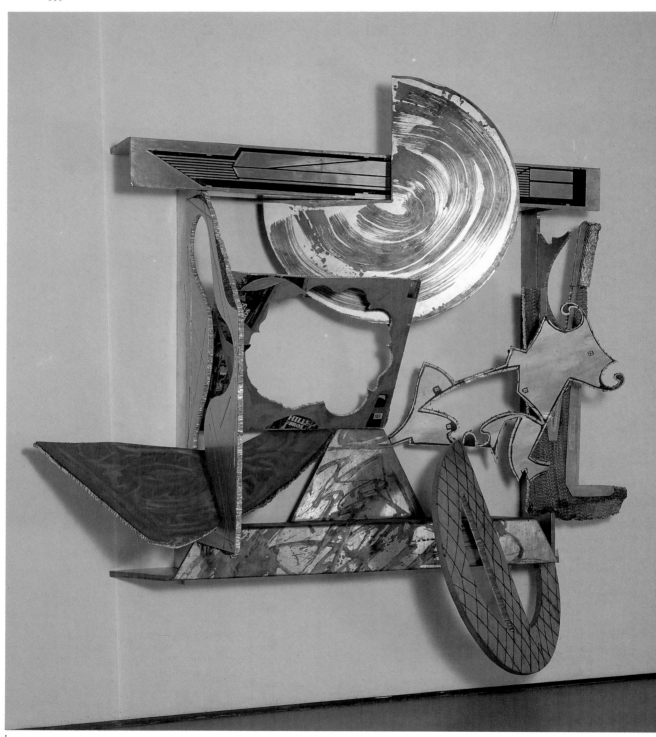

I

2

2
**Walter De Maria
(born Albany, California 1935)**
*A Computer Which Will Solve Every
Problem in the World/3-12 Polygon*, 1984
Stainless polished steel, each 100-cm
length; total area
1900 × 1200 × 100 × 2100 × 300 cm
Purchased 1984; inv. Bek1603
In 1984, at the museum's invitation,
the American artist Walter De Maria
made an impressive floor piece for
the large upstairs gallery in the new
wing, a work conducive to tranquillity and contemplation. Glinting

in the bright light, the 75 stainless-
steel rods are arranged according to
a strict scheme. Starting with a row
of three three-sided rods, the sculpture ends with a row of twelve,
almost round, twelve-sided rods,
each a metre long. This length is a
fixed parameter: the parallel rows
are always a metre apart, and each
succeeding row is one metre longer
in one direction. Notwithstanding
this lucid, serial construction, the
sculpture possesses great visual
complexity, every different vantage
point yielding a new image.

1

1

Joseph Beuys
(Kleve 1921 – Düsseldorf 1986)
Grond, 1980-81
Copper plates and wood, desk, chair,
filing cabinet, loudspeaker, audio
tape, *c*225 × 1200 × 350 cm
Purchased 1981; inv. Bek1579
In this large sculpture, wooden
structures with copper plate cores,
reminiscent of batteries, support a
desk, a chair and a filing cabinet.
The furniture comes from the office
of the owner of the gallery that represented Beuys, René Block, who
closed the premises in 1979 to
become an itinerant organizer of
exhibitions. Beuys arranged the
items into a sculpture which not
only combines forms and materials
but also issues a statement in the
form of a sculpture. Beuys rejected a
narrow, formal definition of art,
opting for an 'expanded concept of
art' whereby anybody can be an
artist because art and life ought to be
fuelled by the same creative energy.
Attached to one of the copper plates
is the 'Aufruf zur Alternative',
Beuys' call for a changed society,
published in the *Frankfurter
Rundschau.* The words *'jetzt brechen
wir den Scheisse ab* (let's get rid of the
shit now)', heard at intervals from
the loudspeaker on one of the con-
structions, express the same senti-
ments. Recorded at the end of an
exhausting *Aktion* in 1968, here the
phrase symbolizes the destruction of
the old forms of art and society and
the beginning of a new future.

2
Sigmar Polke
(born Oels, Silesia 1941)
Das haben wir noch nie so gemacht (We never did it like that before), 1982
Pigment in varnish on cotton,
260 × 200 cm
Purchased 1983; inv. 3068
Depending on how the light falls on the painting, the veils of colour fanning out over the surface have a metallic gleam. The German artist Sigmar Polke often experiments with unconventional pigments and substances in a manner reminiscent of the medieval alchemist. It takes time for the results of his processes to become apparent. Such is the case with this large work, one of a group of three, in which the combination of glue and poppy oil, madder lake and arsenic produces a shade of purple which is still intensifying. Looming up behind the swirling colour are the heads of four cartoon-like figures also featured in *Smithy*, a canvas of 1975. Polke invites the beholder to enter the various layers of the painting, where he is confronted with natural processes and visual clichés, material reality and magic.

3
Anselm Kiefer
(born Donaueschingen 1945)
Dem Unbekannten Maler (To the Unknown Painter), 1982
Oil, lino, straw on linen,
280 × 340 cm
Purchased 1983; inv. 3070

2

3

The first canvases by Penck, Baselitz, Kiefer and Lüpertz came to the museum towards the end of the 1970s. Since then, the work of this generation of artists born mostly in former East Germany during or shortly after the war has formed an important aspect of the collection. With large formats and in an enthusiastically expressionistic vein, they belied the prevalent view that painting has no future. Even more shocking, perhaps, is that, counter to the internationalism of the major trends in art, they explicitly address their own German past. Kiefer links his highly personal interpretations of Germanic myths with historic events in Germany's recent past. The oppressive mood is reinforced by the formats of his canvases, on which he introduces materials like straw, sand and lead, and by the expressive rendering of his often strongly perspectival compositions. Penck, who lived in the GDR until 1980, supplies a pungent, vigorous commentary on politics and society in codes of his own invention. The form of his rudimentary human figures is linked with his interest in primeval times; his alias (his real name is Ralph Winkler) was inspired by the geologist A. R. Penck (1859-1945), whom the artist greatly admires. To Baselitz and Lüpertz, painting is itself the central theme. Faithful to figurative subjects, they focus on abstract problems of painting. Baselitz emphasizes this approach by consistently inverting his motifs. Lüpertz often takes older styles as his point of departure. In the work reproduced here, Baselitz, too, refers to an existing painting: the motif is a version of Edvard Munch's *Arv*, painted in 1897, portraying an ailing mother and her child.

I

2

3

1
Markus Lüpertz
(born Liberec, Bohemia 1941)
Zwischenraumgespenster: Schwarzes
Phantom (Ghosts in Between: Black
Phantom), 1986
Oil on canvas, 200 × 162 cm
Purchased 1987; inv. 3151

2
A. R. Penck
(born Dresden 1939)
Roter Mann (Red Man), 1972
Oil on canvas, 150 × 150 cm
Purchased 1978; inv. 2970

3
Georg Baselitz
(born Deutschbaselitz, Saxony
1938)
1897, 1987
Oil on canvas, 290 × 290 cm
Purchased with support from the
Rembrandt Association 1987;
inv. 3175

3

4

1

1
René Daniels
(born Eindhoven 1950)
Passing in review, 1982
Oil on canvas, 130 × 190 cm
Purchased 1982; inv. 3058

2
Daan van Golden
(born Rotterdam 1936)
Study '86, 1986
Lacquer paint/canvas/plywood,
110 × 86 cm
Purchased 1987; inv. 3143

2

3

**Ger van Elk
(born Amsterdam 1941)**
The Western Stylemasters, 1987
Lacquer paint, colour photograph on
panel, 214 × 131 × 15 cm
Purchased 1987; inv. 3174
Since the late 1960s the Dutch artist
Ger van Elk has chosen widely dif-
fering conventions in art as the point
of departure for works in which he
frequently combines photography
and painting. He also manipulates or
pokes fun at the codes of traditional
genres in painting, such as landscape
and portrait. In *The Western Stylemasters* he engages in dialogue with
the seventeenth-century Dutch
group portrait, venturing a pun by
referring to Rembrandt's famous
Syndics (*Staalmeesters* in Dutch). The
work is distinguished by a pronounced chiaroscuro in which the collars
and cuffs of the two figures (both
self-portraits of the artist) form vivid
accents. The gleaming varnish is
apparently another allusion to
seventeenth-century art, although
the flouting of traditional rules of
composition is undeniably of this
century. The picture, showing the
two figures demonstratively facing
in opposite directions, has a companion piece; painted in the same
year, it shows the men facing each
other, as if conducting a business
transaction.

3

Index